Projects for New Technologies in Education

Grades 6-9

Norma Heller

1994
TEACHER IDEAS PRESS
A Division of
Libraries Unlimited, Inc.
Englewood, Colorado

For Samantha,
with all my love

TEACHER IDEAS PRESS
A Division of
Libraries Unlimited, Inc.
P.O. Box 6633
Englewood, CO 80155-6633
1-800-237-6124

Louisa M. Griffin, Project Editor
Pamela J. Getchell, Design and Layout
Connie Hardesty, Copy Editor
Laura Taylor, Proofreader
Joan Griffitts, Indexer

Library of Congress Cataloging-in-Publication Data

Heller, Norma.
Projects for new technologies in education : grades 6-9 / Norma Heller.
xiv, 154p. 22x28 cm.
Includes bibliographical references and index.
ISBN 1-56308-083-4
1. Educational technology--Handbooks, manuals, etc. 2. Library orientation--Aids and devices--Handbooks, manuals, etc. 3. Research--Data processing--Handbooks, manuals, etc. 4. Middle school libraries--Activity programs--Handbooks, manuals, etc. I. Title.
LB1028.3.H46 1994
371.3'078--dc20 93-44456
CIP

Projects for New Technologies in Education

Contents

List of Tables

Acknowledgments

Grateful acknowledgment is made to New York City Community School Board Eight, and Superintendent Max Messer and his associates. I want to remember the late George Gallego, who had the foresight to purchase computers for the library media center when he was principal. Gary Zaetz, my first computer teacher. Terry Settembre and Assistant Principal Bruce Keltz offered technical assistance. (When nothing worked for me, they were somehow able to push the right button or attach the right cable and, voilà, everything came together.) And the teachers who helped develop the projects in this book: Speech and language teachers Beverly Sims, Amy Alpert, and Lisa Velazquez worked tirelessly with special education students using the *Video Encyclopedia*, proving that hard work and devotion produce results. Rosemary Kerr, whose dedication and love for her students is always paramount, generously shared her copious notes. Teachers Louise Daly and Jeanni Moore were always willing to experiment with new and creative ideas. Teacher Barry Martin was always there to help. Irene Yellin, who first introduced me to the possibilities of studying local history, made endless calls to local politicos to dredge up old maps and photos. And, of course, there are the librarians. Those from the New York City School Library System provided funds, equipment, and training. Susan Hess was always willing to share her time and expertise and first clued me into the possibilities of using commercial information networks with youngsters. Of course, my husband Ira Heller, and my daughters Pamela and Karen, whose encouragement and support kept me going through all those long winter nights! Thank you all for your patience and help.

Introduction

Lessons that integrate the classroom curriculum and library skills have long been recognized as the most effective means of teaching students to use those skills in a variety of learning situations. Advances in technology have made many new and exciting tools available. In *New Technologies for Education: A Beginner's Guide* (Libraries Unlimited, 1993), Ann E. Barron and Gary W. Orwig provide an overview of what technology is now doing. Barron and Orwig discuss the variety of tools (e.g., CD-ROM, videodiscs, and local area networks) that students and instructors can use to access precise, current information and communicate electronically. In this book, you and your students will learn how to apply those tools. One might say that *Projects for New Technologies in Education* is a complement to this 1993 work.

Librarians can teach research skills more effectively than ever before by integrating electronic information resources with the classroom curriculum. For example, *The Video Encyclopedia of the 20th Century* offers a first-hand view into the significant events and people of the past one hundred years, and a CD-ROM electronic encyclopedia takes the tedium out of research by providing information quickly, complete with graphics and sound. However, designing, planning, and implementing interdisciplinary lessons can take an inordinate amount of time, and time is a luxury that most teachers and librarians do not have.

Teaching and simplifying the research process using electronic media is what this book is all about. It offers procedures that can be used by both novice and experienced librarians and teachers. Each chapter focuses on one curriculum subject. The first part of each chapter introduces the curriculum subject and explains how to implement the technology. Then two or more projects are outlined, each with a teaching strategy and reproducible student worksheets.

Why the worksheets? Young teenagers need guidance (although some are ready to work in the abstract, many are not). The worksheets offer precise instructions and examples for using electronic and print resources. The lesson plans allow time for discussion and brainstorming to generate creative solutions to problems. Students then apply their research skills to many kinds of projects that also require the students to use critical thinking skills and to consult with their peers.

The projects in this book make research meaningful and motivate students to use critical thinking skills as they work toward a goal. For example, producing the docudrama (chapter 2) allows students to work together to make critical judgments about selections from the *Video Encyclopedia* and about stories written by their classmates.

Only technology that is basic to student research at the middle school level is used in this book. There is no attempt to use electronic media for special effect or for its own sake. Although research is rarely as neat and orderly as the chapters in this book might indicate, the processes outlined will help to cut through the confusion that often accompanies a research project. The emphasis is on the research process and the use of problem-solving skills.

Many projects in this book are interchangeable and it is not necessary to use each chapter in its entirety. Librarians and teachers can pick and choose projects to suit students' grade levels and abilities, as well as the technologies and time available. Not only are projects interchangeable, so are the kinds of technology used for most of them. Each lesson is broad enough to make use of whatever electronic resources are available and suitable. For example, the debate about immigration (chapter 4) can become the focus of a telecommunications exchange, and one hundred years of heroism (chapter 3) or human behavior and the environment (chapter 6) can become the focus of the debate.

And, of course, the interviews in chapter 8 can be used for the study of immigration. The timetables are estimates only. The number of periods will depend on the number of available computers. Although certain products—HyperCard and WILSONLINE, for example—are used in the teaching plans, any comparable products can be used. A list of products that are used in this book appears in the appendix.

Although the book is limited to communication arts and social studies, many chapters can be expanded to include other subject areas. For example, math teachers might want to have their students tally the results of the community environment survey. Science classes could become involved as well by testing the biodegradability of a variety of products.

Because my experience has been with Apple and Macintosh computers, the book is written with those systems in mind. But, because no instructions are included for the use of the computer, other machines can also be used.

Booktalk to Database: A Student-Created Database of Recommended Books

Students enjoy listening to booktalks and love to be tortured by cliff-hangers. They also love to use computers. This project combines students' enthusiasm for computers with the fun of booktalking. Students read two good books without having to write a book report—an activity that usually is not a kid's idea of fun. Constructing a simple database of recommended reading introduces students to the concept of databases without going online. This is especially useful in school libraries that do not have access to an online service. This chapter includes two projects: one for the booktalks and one for creating the database. Table 1.1 is the timetable of both projects.

Booktalks given by students to their classmates meet myriad goals. Each student must write and memorize a short talk as a sales pitch for the story. Because the talk is very short, it provides even the shyest student an opportunity for public speaking.

The students should choose from many kinds of fiction. To help students select books, make an annotated bibliography or a display of several types of books for students to browse and choose from. I use this opportunity to introduce books that students don't usually check out, but if students object, I allow them to borrow popular titles. However, some control over students' selections must be exercised to ensure variety.

Students who have not recently listened to booktalks should do so before starting this project. This gives them an example to follow that is more effective than written instructions. The first worksheet provides a guide for students. After listening to the booktalks, each student selects a book to read, rate, and add to the database.

The second project in this chapter introduces students to database terminology. The librarian should provide a sample database to be analyzed for content and usefulness. In addition, the librarian should provide instructions for using the database software that students will be using for this project.

In constructing a database, students use problem-solving skills to make cooperative decisions about what information to include and the number of fields to use. They will select headings for each field, such as author, title, student's name, and type of book, avoiding duplicates and understanding the need for precise language. Then, working in groups, each student will enter data into the computer. After each group completes the entries on their books, the file should be printed to show students how each addition enlarges the file.

When all students have entered their data, they should analyze their work and draw conclusions about the data. Who are the most popular authors? What kinds of books received the highest ratings? Which books are preferred by boys? By girls? They should evaluate the file's usefulness and completeness, discuss problems encountered, suggest ways to improve the file, and suggest ideas for other files. Creating and critiquing a database provides skills that will be useful as students go on to create more complex databases or go online to search them. The more classes and grade levels involved in this project, the better the database will be. As books are added and deleted from the original file, students will observe the dynamic nature of a database.

This database should be available in the library media center for students and teachers. It may be distributed to the school district, public libraries, and parents.

Bibliography

Bodart, Joni. *Booktalk! 2: Booktalking for All Ages and Audiences.* New York: H. W. Wilson, 1985.

——. *The New Booktalker.* Vol. 1. Englewood, Colo.: Libraries Unlimited, 1992.

——. *The New Booktalker.* Vol. 2. Englewood, Colo.: Libraries Unlimited, 1993.

——. *100 World-Class Thin Books: Or, What to Read When Your Book Report Is Due Tomorrow.* Englewood, Colo.: Libraries Unlimited, 1993.

Table 1.1
Timetable for Booktalk to Database

Project	Number of Library Periods	Number of Class Periods
Booktalks Worksheet 1.1: Booktalks* Worksheet 1.2: Rating the Book**	1	5
Creating the Database Worksheet 1.3: Understanding Databases Entering data Worksheet 1.4: Evaluating the Database	 2 1 (per group) 1	
Total	4 +1 (per group)	5

*Booktalks may be given in the library or in the classroom, but no more than four or five per period. Each student may choose a book to read after any booktalk. Students should fill out rating sheets and return to the teacher whenever they finish reading their books.

**Rating sheets may be completed as homework.

Teaching Plan I: Booktalks (Worksheets 1.1 and 1.2)

Materials: An annotated bibliography (prepared by the librarian for this project) that includes mysteries, family stories, science fiction, adventure and sports stories as appropriate for the grade or a display of books organized by genre.

Teaching Strategy: The librarian will prepare the class by giving several booktalks. The class will discuss the talks and the use of booktalks to encourage reading. Following the introduction, students will select books for their talks. The teacher or librarian will collect the booktalk forms and check that the correct procedure has been followed and the talk is within the time range of two to three minutes. Students will give booktalks to their classmates (four or five booktalks per session). After listening to classmates' booktalks, students will choose a second book to read. Using worksheet 1.2, they will rate the second book. Data from worksheet 1.2 will be used in the next project, creating the database.

Teaching Plan II: Creating the Database (Worksheets 1.3 and 1.4)

Materials: Sample database; database software, such as PFS: File, Microsoft Works, or Appleworks; computer; printer.

Teaching Strategy: After each student has given a booktalk and has read two books, the librarian will introduce the class to the parts of a database. Definitions of the parts of a database and discussion questions to be used while analyzing the sample database begin this project. The librarian will distribute printouts from sample databases for discussion and analysis. The samples should be from databases created with the software students will use for this project. A sample appears on worksheet 1.3.

Next the librarian will introduce students to the software to be used for this project. The students will learn the terminology and will discuss the information to be included in a database. (I use Microsoft Works in this discussion, but any simple database program can be used.) Students will begin to discuss the information to be included in their database and will determine the headings, the number of fields, and the number and kinds of reports required.

After the class determines the parameters, a group of students will set up the fields, headings, and reports needed. Students will work in groups to enter the data. The database will be printed after each group enters its data; these printouts show how the file changes with each addition.

After the database is complete, students will evaluate it, discussing its usefulness and completeness. Worksheet 1.4 provides some questions to be answered. Following this discussion, fields may be added or deleted. (Keep in mind if a new field is added, that data will need to be entered for each record in the database.) Students should receive a copy of the completed database, and a copy of the printout that was made after their group entered its data.

INTRODUCTION TO BOOKTALKS

You have heard booktalks many times, but have you ever tried to give one? It's not as easy as it looks. To give a booktalk you must read a book very carefully and understand it very well.

For this assignment you will read two books. After reading the first book you will give a booktalk, using the directions that follow. You will choose a second book to read based on a classmate's booktalk. If a book sounds really exciting, choose that book. After you read the second book you will rate it, and we will make a database of all the books using the computer and database software.

A booktalk is a way to interest an audience in a book, and it must be fun for the booktalker and the listeners. To speak enthusiastically about a book you must have enjoyed reading it. Think about how you feel when describing a book, a movie, or a video you thought was great. That is how you should feel about the book you use for your booktalk. Don't use a boring book. Be honest: If you really don't like the first book you choose, try a different one. It's hard to give a booktalk about a book you don't like. The talk should be two to three minutes long. You may memorize it or read it from the worksheet. *Never* tell the ending: The idea is to make your classmates want to read the book. The booktalk should always leave the listeners eager to read the book.

A booktalk always has a beginning, a middle, and a teaser at the end. A booktalk can retell an exciting part of the book or summarize the plot to an exciting moment. You may describe the action: what happens, who does it, and what happens then. Try to create a mood—happy, mysterious, suspenseful, funny—but always leave your audience guessing. *Remember: There must always be a teaser or a cliff-hanger at the end!*

HOW TO GIVE A BOOKTALK

Always start with the title and author of the book. Then hook your audience. The first sentence is the most important. Because the talk is short, you must get your audience's attention immediately and then hold it. The last sentence is also important. You must tell what happens until.... Build suspense and stop just when it becomes unbearable. Always end by repeating the title and author, and always have the book in front of you to show the class.

Based on your booktalk, one of your classmates may decide to read the book you described in your booktalk. That student will be responsible for rating the book and entering information about it into the database.

The following page is a form to help you prepare your booktalk.

Booktalk Form

Name: Class:

Title:

Author:

Type of book (circle one):

Mystery	Science Fiction	Family Story	Sports Story
Teen Romance	Animal Story	Adventure	

Other:

Length of booktalk (minutes):

BOOKTALK

Title:

Author:

Opening sentence:

Body of talk:

Last sentence (cliff-hanger):

Title: Author: Time:

Worksheet 1.2: Rating the Book

As you listen to your classmates' booktalks, select a book that you would like to read. After reading the book fill out this form to rate the book.

Name: Class:

Title:

Author:

Type of book (circle one):

Mystery	Family Story	Animal Story	Sports Story
Science Fiction	Teen Romance	Adventure	

Other:

This booktalk was given by:

I chose this book because:

I gave it the following rating because:

Rating (circle one):

Superior   Very Good   Good   Not Very Good   Poor

Worksheet 1.3: Understanding Databases

A database or data file is a collection of related information that is organized to allow you to find the information you are looking for as easily as possible. For example, a telephone directory is a database of information about people and businesses organized so that you can find what you are looking for quickly and easily.

We are going to make a database of all the books that students in the class read and rated following the booktalks.

GLOSSARY: PARTS OF A DATABASE

File. A database. The telephone directory is a file of everyone who has telephone service in a certain geographical area.

Record. One unit of related pieces of information. For example, the combination of name, address, and telephone number for one person or business is one record in the telephone directory database. (Sample record: Jones, John, 100 Southern Blvd., 988-0042.) When building a database, think of a record as a form to be filled out.

Field. One piece of information within a record. For example, name is a field in each record in the telephone directory. Address is another field, and telephone number is a third field. Think of fields as blanks that must be filled in.

QUESTIONS

1. In a database the most important information is listed first; it is the first field. Why is a person's last name always listed first in the telephone directory?

2. What would happen if the telephone number came first?

On page 7 is a printout from a database used to track overdue library books. Look at the sample, then answer the following questions.

3. Name the fields used for the overdue books list.

4. Why is the class the first field?

5. Why are students' names listed with the last name first?

6. What other information could have been included?

(Worksheet 1.3—continued)

7. Could this database be used for any other purpose if it contained additional information? Explain.

Overdue Library Books—January

Class	Last Name	First Name	Call No.	Copy No.	Title
6SP	Williams	Maria	Fic/D	4A	Doll Hospital
7SP	Morris	Jose	P/M	2	Baby Sitter's #2
7SP	Otero	Lisa	B/J	1A	T. Jefferson
8A1	Abel	Henry	292	3B	Myths Every...
8A1	Fisher	Susan	398	1C	Arabian Nights

USING A DATABASE PROGRAM

A database program allows you to input a great deal of data and then access the information quickly and in any combination you want. For example, you can retrieve records containing only mystery books or books preferred by sixth graders or highly recommended books.

GLOSSARY: PARTS OF A DATABASE PROGRAM

Form. An outline of a record that appears on the screen when you are building a database. A form allows you to enter information one field at a time.

List. A series of items that lets you view information from many different records.

Sort. An option that arranges records in any order you specify. For example, you can sort names in alphabetical order.

Reports. A printout of information from a database. You can create several different reports by combining different pieces of information from a database. In the example of a telephone directory database, name, address, and telephone number is one kind of report; name and telephone number is another kind of report.

CREATING THE DATABASE

When you create a new database, you must create fields and records to contain the information that you want included in the file. Before you can create the fields and records, you must decide the purpose of the database and how it will be used. The following questions will help you plan the structure of your database. Use the information in worksheet 1.2 to decide what fields to include and what to call them.

(Worksheet 1.3—continued)

QUESTIONS

1. What is the purpose of this database?

2. Who is going to use it?

3. What kinds of information do we need to include to make it useful and easy to use?

4. How many fields do we need?

5. What should be the name of each field?

6. What information will need to be included in the reports?

Worksheet 1.4: Evaluating the Database

You should now have two copies of the database, one that was printed after your group completed its data entry and one of the complete database. Answer the following questions.

QUESTIONS

1. Are there enough fields to make this database useful?

2. Should any fields be added or deleted? Which ones and why?

3. Are the fields in the right order, or do we need to change their position?

4. Are the headings useful? How would you change them?

5. What additional reports would be useful?

6. Suggestions for improving the database.

7. Look at the ratings to find out what kinds of books are most popular. Be sure to note the total number of books in the database before you decide which kinds were most popular.

8. From this database can you tell which author is most popular among your classmates?

9. How many of each type of book were read for this project?

Savvy Stories: Using *The Video Encyclopedia of the 20th Century®* to Write a Docudrama

Because kids today grow up in an era of microwaves, 10-second news bites, and MTV, it is frustrating and often impossible to get them to read a novel of any length. We all know kids who first examine the last page of a book to make sure that the number of pages does not exceed two digits. When a book looks too fat or its print too small, it is rejected without another glance. For some time now paperbacks have been one lure for the reluctant reader. A sneaky, often overlooked solution is the short story collection. This tool can not only turn a kid on to reading stories but writing them as well. Just tell the child there is no need to read the whole book—one story will do—and you have taken the first step in converting a nonreader to one who enjoys a good story occasionally. The four projects in this chapter lead students from reading short stories to writing them and finally to creating a videotaped docudrama based on a historical person or event. Table 2.1 is a timetable of the projects.

Young adult anthologies of science fiction, mystery, adventure, and teen romance by outstanding authors are available in most school and public libraries.

The projects in this chapter emphasize both reading and writing stories. Students will work in groups, and each group will write two stories. To begin, students will be introduced to story anthologies and will be allowed to read any story. Have them scan the table of contents of an anthology to find a story that looks good. When the students understand that you are asking them to read only 10 or 12 pages, you will see smiles spread from ear to ear. You will be rewarded when they return the following week to say that they really enjoyed finding out what happened in the story without having to read a whole lot of junk. These kids will come back later, asking for more stories by Edgar Allan Poe or Ray Bradbury or Isaac Asimov.

After students have read one or more stories of their own choosing and listened to the teacher or librarian read some stories aloud, the teacher will assign stories to be read for a comparison of writing styles. By comparing and contrasting writing styles, students begin to understand how authors use character and setting to pique and hold readers' interest. Students will analyze how writers use dialogue to convey a point of view. They will begin to make evaluations about what constitutes good writing and develop standards to use in their own writing. After reading, listening to, and discussing stories by many authors, students will write the first group story.

The teacher will divide the class into groups. Each group will write a story to be read aloud, evaluated by other groups, revised, and completed. Working in small groups allows students to synthesize ideas. Students develop problem-solving skills as they participate in deciding what works and why and discarding unworkable ideas. In addition, the process gives students insight into themselves and others, which fosters mutual respect and understanding. Writing, critiquing, and revising stories will encourage students to keep reading and to pay attention to the effective use of language as they get ready for the second writing assignment.

The Video Encyclopedia of the 20th Century is a wonderful motivational tool that includes more than 40 laser discs with a total of more than 2,000 film clips of events that took place during the last one hundred years. All the film clips are original material with no added commentary, music, or sound effects. They provide vast amounts of information and allow students to see events and form mental images. When used as part of a writing project, the *Video Encyclopedia* is an exciting and stimulating tool that gives students a broad picture of life during a particular period of history. Students can use a historic event in a story plot or setting.

Drawing on segments of the *Video Encyclopedia* for ideas enlivens writing and encourages students to read additional stories or to research another era. Tell students that this is the stuff of television and motion picture docudramas, which are based on historic events and people combined with fictionalized characters.

Students will use the *Video Encyclopedia* index and reference volumes for information about the film clips and will choose clips that interest them. They

Table 2.1
Timetable for Savvy Stories

Project	Number of Library Periods	Number of Class Periods
Introducing Short Stories		
Worksheet 2.1: Parts of a Story Collection	1	
Worksheet 2.2: Reading Short Stories		2
Writing the First Group Story		
Worksheet 2.3: Types of Stories	1	3
Worksheet 2.4: Writing the First Group Story	4 (per group)	4
Learning to Use the *Video Encyclopedia*		
Worksheet 2.5: Using *The Video Encyclopedia of the 20th Century**	2	
Selecting Film Clips		
Worksheet 2.6: Selecting the Film Clips	4 (per group)	
Worksheet 2.7: Writing the Group Story	2 (per group)	4
Producing the Docudrama		
Worksheet 2.8: Producing the Docudrama	5	2
Total	9 +10 (per group)	15

*Worksheet 2.5: Number of periods depends on the number of index volumes available.

will use critical thinking skills to analyze the film segments for use in story plots; they may combine elements from a variety of segments into a story. Students are able to see and hear Amelia Earhart and then write a story about her disappearance; they can watch President and Mrs. Roosevelt entertain the King and Queen of England in 1939. They can imagine what it would be like to accompany the astronauts into space, or to be at Kitty Hawk with the Wright brothers. As students become excited about these characters and events they will apply what they have learned about short story writing to develop characters, plots, and settings. They will use problem-solving skills to decide which film clips can be developed into a story. They will learn about history even as they practice writing short stories.

Students will write group stories based on film segments of their choosing. They will write, revise, and print the stories using a computer. They will evaluate each other's stories and choose one to be made into a videotaped docudrama. All stories can be collected for use in an anthology that will become part of the school library collection.

Bibliography

Short Stories

Aiken, Joan. *Up the Chimney Down & Other Stories*. New York: Harper & Row, 1984. Fantasy and many eccentric characters in these 11 stories.

Asimov, Isaac, ed. *Young Witches and Warlocks*. New York: Harper & Row, 1987.

——. *Young Star Travelers*. New York: Harper & Row, 1986.

——. *Young Monsters*. New York: Harper & Row, 1985.

——. *Young Ghosts*. New York: Harper & Row, 1985.

——. *Young Mutants*. New York: Harper & Row, 1984. Popular science fiction collections featuring youthful protagonists of all kinds. Authors include Andre Norton, Arthur C. Clarke, and Ray Bradbury.

Brittain, Bill. *The Wish Giver*. New York: Harper & Row, 1983. Three magical stories.

Cameron, Peter. *One Way or Another*. New York: Harper & Row, 1986. Stories about young people and their confrontations with the pain of loss, betrayal, and abandonment.

Cohen, Daniel. *The Restless Dead*. New York: Dodd, Mead, 1984. Scary stories from many countries.

Cormier, Robert. *Eight Plus One*. New York: Pantheon Books, 1980. Stories that deal with relationships and emotions.

Conford, Ellen. *If This Is Love, I'll Take Spaghetti*. New York: Four Winds Press, 1983. Stories that capture the feelings and struggles of adolescents.

Fleischman, Paul. *Graven Images*. New York: Harper & Row, 1982. Three stories of the supernatural. A Newbery Honor Book.

Gallo, Donald, ed. *Visions*. New York: Delacorte Press, 1987.

——. *Sixteen: Short Stories by Outstanding Writers*. New York: Delacorte Press, 1984. Stories by outstanding writers about the problems of the teen years.

Girion, Barbara. *A Very Brief Season*. New York: Macmillan, 1984. Stories dealing with emotions and events in the lives of teenagers.

Hill, Donna. *Eerie Animals*. New York: Atheneum, 1983. Supernatural tales about unusual animals.

Hoke, Helen, ed. *Horrifying & Hideous Hauntings: An Anthology*. New York: E. P. Dutton, 1986. Ghost stories by authors including Ray Bradbury, Joan Aiken, and Dorothy Sayers.

Holtzman, Jerome, ed. *Fielder's Choice*. New York: Harcourt Brace Jovanovich, 1979. For all sports enthusiasts, baseball stories from authors including Ring Lardner and James Thurber.

Huggins, Isabel. *The Elizabeth Stories*. New York: Viking, 1984. Wonderful interwoven stories about growing up in Ontario, Canada.

Ireson, Barbara. *In a Class of Their Own*. Boston: Faber & Faber, 1985. Stories dealing with school days past, present, and future.

Kahn, Joan., ed. *Handle with Care: Frightening Stories*. New York: Greenwillow Books, 1985.

——. *Ready or Not, Here Comes Fourteen Frightening Stories*. New York: Greenwillow Books, 1987.

Kennedy, Richard. *Collected Stories*. New York: Harper & Row, 1987. Wonderfully imaginative stories with the magic of folktales. Great for reading aloud.

Lester, Julius. *This Strange New Feeling*. New York: Dial Press, 1982. Love stories set at the time of slavery. All based on true stories.

Segal, Elizabeth, comp. *Short Takes*. New York: Lothrop, Lee & Shepard, 1986. Stories for younger readers about the trials of growing up.

Yolen, Jane, Martin Greenberg, and Charles Waugh, eds. *Dragons and Dreams*. New York: Harper & Row, 1984. Science fiction and fantasy by such authors as Jane Yolen and Zilpha Keatley Snyder.

Books About Writing

Asher, Sand. *Where Do You Get Your Ideas?* New York: Walker, 1987.

Cassedy, Sylvia. *In Your Own Words*. New York: Doubleday, 1987.

Dubrovin, Vivian. *Write Your Own Story*. New York: Franklin Watts, 1984.

Teaching Plan I: Introducing Short Stories (Worksheets 2.1 and 2.2)

Materials: A variety of short story anthologies for young adults, class set of a paperback anthology.

Teaching Strategy: Students will be encouraged to read many short stories from a variety of collections and will listen to the teacher and librarian read stories aloud. Worksheet 2.1 will introduce students to the parts of an anthology.

Next, students will be introduced to the basic parts of a story: characters, plot, dialogue, point of view, and setting. The teacher will give each student a paperback story collection, such as Gallo's *Visions* or *Sixteen* (see bibliography on this page). The teacher will assign two stories to be read, and students will compare setting, characters, point of view, dialogue, and plot.

Teaching Plan II: Writing the First Group Story (Worksheets 2.3 and 2.4)

Materials: Computer, word processing software, printer, short story bibliography (pages 11-12), and short story anthologies.

Teaching Strategy: Students will become familiar with different types of stories. The teacher may want to provide copies of the same story to the entire class. Students will begin writing assignments, working in groups, with each group writing a different kind of story.

Students will be provided with exercises to help them get started (see worksheet 2.4). They will begin work on the group stories, writing the details of the plot, characters, and setting. Each group will use the computer to write and revise its story. The final copy will be presented to each of the other groups to read, discuss, evaluate, and offer constructive criticism. Revisions will be made until each group completes its story.

Teaching Plan III: Learning to Use *The Video Encyclopedia of the 20th Century* (Worksheet 2.5)

Materials: *The Video Encyclopedia of the 20th Century*: laser discs, reference and index volumes; laser disc player; VCR; television monitor; and worksheet 2.5.

Teaching Strategy: The librarian will explain the time period covered by the *Video Encyclopedia* and the kinds of film segments it includes. The librarian will demonstrate the use of the *Video Encyclopedia*. Students will use the exercises on worksheet 2.5 to become familiar with the reference and index volumes.

Teaching Plan IV: Selecting Film Clips (Worksheets 2.6 and 2.7)

Materials: *The Video Encyclopedia of the 20th Century*: laser discs, reference and index volumes; 5-by-7-inch index cards; computer; word processing software; VCR; television monitor; worksheets 2.6 and 2.7.

Teaching Strategy: Students will be grouped by the time period in which they are interested. They will use the index and reference volumes as sources for story ideas and will begin to select film clips to use in their stories. They will view the clips they select, discussing, analyzing, evaluating, discarding, and making final selections of the film clips they intend to use.

The librarian will demonstrate the procedure used to videotape the laser discs and will hand out copies of the instructions (see page 28). All the selected film clips will be videotaped to provide easy access for student review.

Students will begin to write stories, using both real and imaginary characters based on the events depicted in the film clips. Students will use the computer to write, revise, and print their stories. An anthology of the stories should be compiled and added to the school library's short story collection. This volume should include a title page, table of contents, publication date, introduction, and biographical notes about the authors.

Teaching Plan V: Producing the Docudrama (Worksheet 2.8)

Materials: Video camera, VCR, television monitor, blank videotapes, editing equipment, worksheet 2.8.

Teaching Strategy: Only one story will be written as a docudrama and videotaped. Each group will read and evaluate the stories written by every other group. Criteria for the selection of the story to be dramatized should include how effectively the dialogue portrays the characters and the time in which they lived, the level of interest in the historical event, the level of suspense and resolution of the conflict, and how imaginatively the real and fictionalized parts of the story are interwoven.

After one story is selected, the group that wrote the original story will rewrite it as a screenplay with as few changes as possible. Students will be selected for acting, directing, and using the equipment. Copies of the script will be distributed to participating students, a rehearsal schedule will be set, and the play will be videotaped. The videotape should be added to the library collection and shown to parent groups and district personnel. For instructions about writing a play see chapter 5.

Worksheet 2.1: Parts of a Story Collection

A short story anthology or collection consists of many stories selected by an editor or compiler. The stories in an anthology have something in common. They may be written by one author or may be a specific kind of story, such as mystery or science fiction. They may come from one country or a certain period of history, or winners of a certain prize may be collected and published in one volume.

GLOSSARY: PARTS OF A STORY COLLECTION

Editor or compiler. The person who selects the stories to be included in an anthology.

Title page. The page bearing the title of the collection, editor or compiler, publisher, city, and year of publication.

Table of contents. A list of the stories in the collection, including the title, author, and page on which each story begins.

Introduction. A passage in which the editor or compiler explains why certain stories were selected for the collection and discusses the background of the authors.

Author. The person who wrote one or more stories included in the anthology.

Biographical notes. A section in which the editor summarizes biographical information about each author featured in the anthology and lists other stories written by the author.

Blurb. A brief passage on the inside front cover or on the back of the book that summarizes what kinds of stories and authors are included in the collection.

USING A STORY COLLECTION

Select an anthology from the school library's short story collection and complete the following information.

Title of the collection:

Name of editor or compiler:

Publisher and year of publication:

Kind of anthology (mystery, science fiction, horror, ghost story, or other):

Select several stories to read from this or a different anthology found in the school library.

Worksheet 2.2: Reading Short Stories

GLOSSARY: PARTS OF A STORY

Character. Persons or actors in a story. A short story usually has one main character and a number of less important characters.

Plot. The story line or line of action. What problem does the main character face? Usually, the problem is introduced at the beginning of the story, unfolds in the middle, and is resolved at the end. This is the *resolution*. The *climax* is the most exciting part of the story.

Setting. Where and when the story takes place.

Dialogue. Conversation among characters. A reader can use dialogue to understand the characters by paying careful attention to what is said, how it is said, how the character feels, and the kind of person the character is.

Point of view. Who is telling the story. Three points of view are:

First person: "I" (I saw the man at the top of the stairs and ran for my life.)

Third person: "He" or "She" (He saw the man at the top of the stairs.)

All-knowing: Involved with all the action. (The boy saw the man at the top of the stairs, and the man knew how scared the boy was.)

READING STORIES

Read the two stories that have been assigned by your teacher. Use the following questions to compare the features of each story.

Story One

Title:

Author:

(Describe the following.)

Main character:

Setting:

Plot (What is the problem the main character faces, and how is it solved?):

Point of view (circle one): First Person Third Person All-knowing

Dialogue (Give an example of how the dialogue helps you understand the main character.):

(Worksheet 2.2—continued)

Story Two

Title:

Author:

(Describe the following.)

Main character:

Setting:

Plot (What is the problem the main character faces, and how is it solved?):

Point of view (circle one): First Person Third Person All-knowing

Dialogue (Give an example of how the dialogue helps you understand the main character.):

COMPARING THE STORIES

Main Character

1. In which story does the main character seem more real?

2. What words does the author use to make the main character real to you?

3. In which story do you like the main character better? Why?

(Worksheet 2.2—continued)

Setting

1. Describe and compare the setting of each of the two stories.

2. Explain how the description of the setting helps you understand the characters or adds to the mood of the stories.

Plot

1. Compare the plots of the stories. Tell what the problem was, how it was resolved, and describe the climax.

2. If you enjoyed one story more than the other, explain why.

3. Which story kept you reading and eager to find out how the problem would be solved? Explain why.

Point of View

1. Compare the point of view used in each story. If they differ, tell which point of view you liked better and why.

Dialogue

1. How did the dialogue in each story help you understand the characters and plot?

Worksheet 2.3: Types of Stories

The following kinds of stories are among the types usually found in short story collections for teenagers.

Fantasy—Stories about imaginary worlds full of magic and strange creatures that we know cannot possibly exist on Earth.

Science Fiction—Modern fantasies that combine the real world and the world of the future or reality and fantasy. Science fiction is based on the scientific knowledge of today and scientific predictions of the future. These predictions sometimes come true in our lifetimes. Ask yourself "what if," and think about machines that can do incredible things.

Ghost Story—A type of fantasy story featuring ghosts and ghostly happenings, haunted houses, and haunted objects.

Mystery—Stories of crime and detection. Sometimes the murderer is known right from the beginning, but that need not detract from the excitement of the pursuit and capture. Sometimes you do not know the name of the criminal until the final page, and you are led along trying to guess "whodunit" until the very end.

Adventure—Stories with lots of action in which the hero must overcome a dangerous situation.

Realism—Stories based on real problems of everyday lives. These stories can take place in the past or present.

READING VARIOUS TYPES OF STORIES

Choose a story collection from the bibliography the teacher gave to the class and read one story of each type listed below. For each story you read, list the collection title, story title, and the author of the story.

Fantasy

Science Fiction

Ghost Story

Mystery

Adventure

Realism

Other

Setting

Compare the setting of each story. List the words that the authors use to set the mood of the story.

Fantasy:

Science Fiction:

Ghost Story:

(Worksheet 2.3—continued)

Mystery:

Adventure:

Realism:

Other:

Writing a Setting

Describe a setting for a...

Fantasy:

Science Fiction:

Ghost Story:

Mystery:

Adventure:

Realism:

Other:

Worksheet 2.4: Writing the First Group Story

Now that you have read many different kinds of stories and compared various settings, characters, plots, and dialogue, it's time to start writing. Each group of students will write a different kind of story. After the class discusses the kinds of stories everybody wants to write, form a group with other students who want to write the same kind of story that you want to write.

WRITING EXERCISES: USING YOUR SENSES

Your writing becomes vivid and your characters and settings come alive when you use your senses to describe them. To write a story that people want to read, you must observe the world around you carefully. Sometimes it helps to keep a notebook and write things down as you observe them. Write a few sentences in your notebook using each of the following senses. This will help you become a better observer.

Sight

1. Close your eyes and visualize your room at home. Write down all the details you can remember.
2. Describe your best friend.
3. Remember an interesting person you knew once and write a description.
4. Compare something you see with something else that looks like it.

Hearing

1. What does the school cafeteria sound like?
2. What noises do you hear outside your classroom right now?
3. Listen to people talking. What are they saying? How would you describe their voices?
4. Describe the sounds you hear on a crowded bus. In a movie theater.
5. Describe the different voices you hear on a TV news show.
6. Describe the sounds made by your favorite cereal.
7. Remember a recent conversation between a family member and you. Write it down.

(Worksheet 2.4—continued)

Touch

1. Close your eyes and have a friend hold an object out to you. Describe how it feels.

2. How do your blue jeans feel? How does silk or velvet feel?

3. How does it feel to walk on hot sand without shoes?
4. Describe how shaving cream or whipped cream feels.

Smell

1. Describe the smells of the school lunchroom on a good day.
2. Describe your favorite meal.
3. How do a new lipstick, a brand new book, or a chocolate bar smell?

Taste

1. Close your eyes and have a friend put something that tastes good in your mouth. Describe it.

2. Describe a juicy cheeseburger and fries.
3. Remember a medication you had to take when you were sick. How did it taste?

Combine the Senses

1. Write a description using all your senses.

START YOUR STORY

Begin to work on your story one element at a time. You have already practiced setting. Now work on the characters, plot, setting, dialogue, and point of view to be used in your group story.

Using your imagination, brainstorm with your group to detail how the characters in your story look and sound, including how they walk and sit, their posture, their gestures, how they look when they smile, frown, or laugh. The type and color of their clothing should be included. How would you describe their personalities: depressed, happy, gloomy, cheerful, outgoing, shy? What makes them that way? What kinds of voices do your characters have? Do they speak softly or scream? Do they speak harshly or quietly? Why? What makes them behave as they do? Remember every character should be different. (You will need to outline your story and answer the following questions on a separate sheet of paper.)

(Worksheet 2.4—continued)

Setting

Brainstorm the details of the setting. What kind of setting is best for the kind of story you are going to write? When does the story take place? Where? What's the weather like? What season is it? Is the place crowded, lonely, indoors or out? Does your main character feel comfortable there? If not, why not? Is it a quiet or noisy place, clean or messy?

Plot

Outline the plot with your group. What will the problem be? How will you grab your readers' interest right at the beginning? What will be the climax or most exciting part of the story? How will the problem be resolved?

Dialogue

Dialogue attempts to reveal characters' personalities as well as the problem. The way characters talk to each other tells a great deal about them. What is the mood of the people speaking? Are they honest? Do they say what they mean? How can you describe what the characters are saying to reveal what they are really thinking?

Point of View

Will this story be told from the point of view of the main character or the narrator? Will the narrator be all-knowing? Remember, there can be only one voice in a story.

Putting It All Together

Use the computer in the library or classroom to write and revise your story.

Worksheet 2.5: Using The Video Encyclopedia of the 20th Century

The Video Encyclopedia of the 20th Century includes over 40 laser discs with a total of more than 2,000 film clips of events that have taken place over the last one hundred years. The film clips feature people as well as historic events. There are film clips of former presidents, movie stars, fashion shows, astronauts, sports events, world figures, natural disasters, war battles, and much more.

THE INDEX VOLUME

The table that follows will help you learn to find information on the *Video Encyclopedia*. Use the index to find the subjects listed. Write in the missing information next to each subject. If there is more than one reference choose only one. The first one has been done for you.

Subject	Reference Number	Laser Disc Number	Side/ Chapter	Length of Clip	Video/ Audio
Spitfire	1924	29	B/14	1:04	b&w/sil
Chess					
Cruise, Tom					
Archery					
Tacoma Narrows Bridge					
Ruby, Jack					
Haircuts					
Earthquakes					

(Worksheet 2.5—continued)

USING THE REFERENCE VOLUMES

The reference volumes give detailed information about each film clip. This exercise will help you learn to use them. Use the reference volumes to look up each subject under its reference number. Remember, you looked up the reference number for each subject in the previous exercise. Using information from the reference volumes, fill in the following form. The first one has been done for you.

Subject	Reference Number	Unit Title	Year of Event	People Featured on Film Clip	Short Summary
Spitfire	1924	...In the Battle of Britain	1940	Pilots of the Spitfire	WWII Spitfire in action.
Chess					
Cruise, Tom					
Archery					
Tacoma Narrows Bridge					
Ruby, Jack					
Haircuts					
Earthquakes					

Worksheet 2.6: Selecting the Film Clips

A docudrama is a play based on a historical person or event with imaginary characters and events added to the story to make history more personal. You are going to write stories based on actual events and real people featured in film clips that you choose from the *Video Encyclopedia*. One of the stories will be dramatized as a docudrama. Use your imagination to add fictional characters (or yourself) to the story. You may write any kind of story you like—mystery or science fiction, for example—and you may use as many historic events as you like. You may even change history—but remember, there must be a real event and a real person involved. You will work in a group of five or six to write the story.

CHOOSING FILM CLIPS

Select a period of the twentieth century and select the kinds of events or people you are most interested in writing about. Some possibilities are hurricanes, the assassination of President John F. Kennedy, Amelia Earhart's historic flights, automobile racing, submarines, volcanoes, sports, space flight and exploration, women's suffrage or World War II.

If you are unable to think of a subject that interests you, browse through the index volume of the *Video Encyclopedia* to find one.

RECORDING THE INFORMATION

On 5-by-7-inch index cards, record important information about each film clip. Use a separate card for each clip. The information needed can be found in the *Video Encyclopedia* index and reference volumes. Following is an example of how your card might look. You may arrange your card differently, but be sure to include all the information asked for on this sample.

Index Card

Subject____

Reference number__________ Laser disc number_______ Side/Chapter number__________

Length of clip__________ Video/Audio__________

Unit title______________________________ Year__________

People featured on the film clip______________________________

____

Short summary____________________________________

____

____

____

Worksheet 2.7: Writing the Group Story

With the librarian's permission, select and stack all the laser discs that you will be using. Brainstorm with your group the possibilities of combining the real people and events on the film clips that you listed on the index cards with imaginary characters and events. Write down all of the ideas. View each of the selected film clips. Use the following questions to help you brainstorm. Use the back of the worksheet or additional sheets of paper if there is not enough space for your answers.

QUESTIONS

1. Describe what is happening in this film clip.

2. Describe the people on the film clip.

3. How would it feel to be a bystander at a historic event?
4. Describe what would happen if someone or something else were present during the event depicted on the film clip.

5. Describe how the presence of this imaginary person or thing would affect this event.

6. What does this imaginary person look like?

7. How would you have reacted to this event if you were present?

8. Imagine a problem that could have occurred at the time of the event in the film clip—a problem that no one but your imaginary character was aware of. How could it be solved?

Discard the index cards for the clips you will not use. If additional information is needed to write the story, use reference material available in the library to research the event, the people involved, the era in which the event took place, and other events that took place during the same time period. Videotape all of the clips your group decides to use. Instructions for making a videotape appear on page 28.

(Worksheet 2.7—continued)

WRITING THE STORY

If you haven't already done so, decide what kind of story to write. Use the film clips and the brainstorming notes. Did the group select film clips that would make the basis of a good science fiction or fantasy story, or would it be best to make this a realistic story? Decide which student will write each part of the story, and then divide the following assignments among members of the group:

- Write descriptions of all the real and imaginary characters. If you are in the story, write a description of yourself as well.
- Write about a problem, real or imaginary, that could have happened or did happen at the time depicted in the film clips. What was the conflict? How was it resolved? How do the characters react to the problem?
- Write dialogue among the real and imaginary characters. When the story is dramatized, the dialogue will be the most important part. The dialogue should tell what the problem is, how the characters feel about each other and the problem, what the conflict, is, and how the characters will go about resolving it.

Be sure to describe the setting so that readers will understand when and where this event took place. When the story is dramatized, a narrator can explain the setting to the viewers.

Use the videotape of the selected film clips to remind you of the event and the characters involved.

Use the computer in your classroom or library to write your story and to make all revisions.

Instructions for Making a Videotape from The Video Encyclopedia of the 20th Century

Viewing film clips from many different laser discs takes lots of time. To see several clips many times, it is easier to videotape the clips from the laser discs and view them on videotape as needed. This is lots of fun and very easy. Follow these instructions carefully.

1. Stack the laser discs in the order in which you will record them.
2. Turn on the television monitor, VCR, and laser disc player. Be sure that the television and VCR are on channel 3.
3. Using the laser disc player remote control, press Eject once. Place the first laser disc on the tray.
4. Press Chapter on the laser disc remote control and enter the number of the chapter.
5. Press Search on the laser disc remote control.
6. When the picture appears on the screen, press Record on the VCR. *Do not use the VCR remote control. Be careful not to record the chapter numbers as they appear on the screen.*
7. When the film clip is copied, press Pause on the VCR.
8. Repeat this procedure for each film clip you wish to copy. NOTE: It is not necessary to use the Record button on the VCR again. Just press Pause to stop, and press it again to restart recording.
9. When you are done taping, remove the last laser disc. Press Play on the laser disc remote control to close the disc tray.
10. View the tape made from the laser discs. Check each clip as it appears on the screen to be sure that the chapter number does not appear and that you recorded the whole clip.

Worksheet 2.8: Producing the Docudrama

The whole class will decide which story will be dramatized. Exchange stories with every group. Evaluate the stories based on the following criteria:

- Are there both real and imaginary characters in the story?
- Does the event interest a large group of people?
- Did you learn anything new and exciting about this event?
- Does the dialogue present the characters' points of view effectively? Is there dialogue between the real and imaginary characters?
- How exciting is the story? Is there a real conflict presented and resolved?
- Is the real event interwoven imaginatively with the fictionalized part of the story?

Stories use dialogue and descriptions of characters, setting, and action. A play uses dialogue but relies on the stage to show characters, setting, and action. Because we are not going to build scenery or use costumes, we will use a narrator to describe the setting. When you rewrite your story, don't change the dialogue among the characters, but add stage directions to tell the actors how to express feelings with gestures, facial expressions, and general body language. All stage directions are written in the script but are not spoken. (You might write them in parentheses to set them apart from the dialogue). Stage directions tell actors what to do at any given time.

One Hundred Years of Heroism: A Videotaped Report

Sensational stories about instant celebrities dominate the news these days. Fame is granted to notorious, sometimes disreputable, people whose sordid misdeeds assume grand importance through daily media coverage. These figures are soon forgotten only to be replaced by more lurid figures. Gossip is hot and we all seem to have turned into back-fence busybodies.

We don't seem to hear much about true heroes: men and women whose greatness encourages us to strive for goals that we might otherwise consider unattainable. However, the twentieth century has produced many men and women of great courage who are self-sacrificing and extraordinary, whose exploits provide worthy inspiration for youngsters. As the century's end nears, it is time to look back to see which people made a difference in our lives and the lives of others, perhaps changing the course of history.

Who are the heroes of the twentieth century? What are the qualities of personality or character that make them so outstanding? What have they accomplished? What makes them different from everyone else? Are heroes born with some special gift, or do the circumstances of their lives drive them toward their special destinies? Does fate play a part, by placing them at a time in history when an event makes them act in a way that is different from those around them? Whether these men and women are scientists, civil rights leaders, sports figures, or inventors, they are people who believed deeply and whose deeds made a difference. It is important to make these heroes familiar to students; to fuel their imaginations and fantasies and to encourage them to emulate these extraordinary people.

This chapter focuses on understanding the characteristics of heroes. Four projects are included: Legendary Heroes, Twentieth Century Heroes, Using *The Video Encyclopedia of the 20th Century*, and Making Videotape (of twentieth century heroes). Table 3.1 is a timetable of all four projects.

Students will begin by reading stories about legendary heroes. (See bibliography.) They will learn how these heroes personified the qualities that were exalted by a particular people at a particular time in history, and they will compare and contrast these qualities with those of real-life heroes. They will discuss the qualities of character that are glorified in our society and understand how our heroes are often molded to fit those characteristics.

Students will discuss the difference between a hero and a role model, and they will agree to a definition of *hero* to use for this project. Each student, or a group of students working together, will choose an outstanding leader of the twentieth century and write a report about that person. For research, students will read biographies and use reference sources, including biographical dictionaries and *Current Biography*. Using the definition agreed upon, the class will discuss the special qualities of these men and women and decide whether they meet the definition.

Next, students will be introduced to *The Video Encyclopedia of the 20th Century*. The *Video Encyclopedia* allows students to see, and sometimes hear, people they have read about. Students will see their heroes come alive and understand more fully why these people may be considered heroes. All the students will view chosen film clips, but only an elected group of students will videotape the film clips of their heroes based on worksheet 3.5 and the written reports. Selected students will synthesize the material from their reading with material from the *Video Encyclopedia* to make an audio component that explains why each person included on the videotape was chosen. A final videotaped discussion will be based on a script in which all participants defend their selections.

Bibliography

Blair, Walter. *Tall Tale America*. Chicago: University of Chicago Press, 1987. Humorous heroes from American folklore.

Bruchac, Joseph. *Iroquois Stories*. Trumansburg, N.Y.: Crossing Press, 1985. Heroes and heroines from Iroquois legends.

Table 3.1
Timetable for One Hundred Years of Heroism

Project	Number of Library Periods	Number of Class Periods
Legendary Heroes		
Worksheet 3.1: Epic Heroes	1	1
Twentieth Century Heroes		
Worksheet 3.2: Defining *Hero*	2	
Worksheet 3.3: Biographies and Biographical Sources	3	
Worksheet 3.4: Taking Notes	2	2
Using the *Video Encyclopedia*		
Worksheet 3.5: Using the *Video Encyclopedia**	2 (per group)	2
Making the Videotape		
Worksheet 3.6: Making the Videotape	4	
Total	12 +2 (per group)	5

*Although students may work individually, it may be necessary to use the *Video Encyclopedia* in groups because of the limited number of laser disc players and *Video Encyclopedia* indexes and reference books.

Colum, Padraic. *The Golden Fleece and the Heroes Who Lived before Achilles*. New York: Macmillan, 1983. The cycle of myths about the Argonauts and the quest for the Golden Fleece as well as other tales.

Courlander, Harold. *The Heart of the Ngoni: Heroes of the African Kingdom of Segu*. New York: Crown, 1982. African legends.

Fadiman, Clifton. *The Story of Young King Arthur*. New York: Random House, 1961. Arthur's early years from youth to marriage.

Gibson, Michael. *Gods, Men and Monsters from the Greek Myths*. New York: Schocken Books, 1982. Exploits and adventures of heroes from ancient Greece.

Hodges, Margaret. *Saint George and the Dragon*. New York: Little, Brown, 1984. Retells the segment from Spenser's *Faerie Queen* in which George slays the dragon that has been terrorizing the countryside.

Hutton, Warren. *Theseus and the Minotaur*. New York: Macmillan, 1989. Lovely illustrations help to tell the story of how Theseus risked his life and slayed the Minotaur.

Knappert, Jan. *Kings, Gods and Spirits from African Mythology*. New York: Schocken Books, 1986. A collection of African myths, legends, and fables.

Oakden, David. *Legends and Heroes*. New York: Rourke, 1982. Norse and Greek myths.

Richardson, Donald. *Greek Mythology for Everyone: Legends of the Gods and Heroes*. New York: Avenel, 1989. Gods and heroes from Greece.

Riordan, James. *An Illustrated Treasury of Myths and Legends*. New York: Bedrick Books, 1991. International collection of 25 tales of courage, including Robin Hood, El Cid, and Perseus.

——. *The Women in the Moon and Other Tales of Forgotten Heroines*. New York: Dial Press, 1984. Traditional tales from around the world.

Saxby, H. M. *The Great Deeds of Superheroes*. New York: Bedrick Books, 1990. Legendary, mythological, and religious heroes, including El Cid, Roland, Moses, Samson, Sigurd, Gilgamesh, and many others.

Thompson, Vivian L. *Hawaiian Tales of Heroes and Champions*. Honolulu: University of Hawaii Press, 1986. Legends from Hawaii.

Usher, Kerry. *Heroes, Gods and Emperors from Roman Mythology*. New York: Schocken Books, 1984. Myths and life in ancient Rome.

Wood, Marion. *Spirits, Heroes and Hunters from North American Indian Mythology*. New York: Schocken Books, 1982. Native American myths and legends.

Teaching Plan I: Legendary Heroes (Worksheet 3.1)

Materials: Bibliography that features legends and epic heroes (pages 30-31).

Teaching Strategy: The communication arts teacher and the librarian will introduce the class to legends and myths using stories about heroes who personify the ideals of a nation at a particular time in history. Questions to be answered after the stories are read appear on worksheet 3.1. The class will discuss the ways in which legendary heroes compare to real-life heroes.

Teaching Plan II: Twentieth Century Heroes (Worksheets 3.2, 3.3, and 3.4)

Materials: Completed worksheet 3.1, a variety of dictionaries and biographical reference sources, the index to *Current Biography* and copies of the periodical, a list of people from *The Video Encyclopedia of the 20th Century*, index to the *Video Encyclopedia*.

Teaching Strategy: The students will compare and contrast legendary heroes with twentieth century heroes. Based on the definition of *hero*, the students will decide what kind of people will be considered for this project. In a class discussion, the students will define *hero*, applying what they have read about epic heroes. Students will distinguish between a hero and a role model.

A list of some of the people who appear on the *Video Encyclopedia* appears on worksheet 3.2; students will choose an individual and will write a biographical report about that person. Additional names may be found by searching the index to the *Video Encyclopedia*. They should find as much biographical information as they can, using many different kinds of biographical reference sources, including *Current Biography* and biographical dictionaries. Worksheets 3.3 and 3.4 will guide them through this part of the project.

Teaching Plan III: Using the Video Encyclopedia (Worksheet 3.5)

Materials: *The Video Encyclopedia of the 20th Century*: laser discs, reference and index volumes; VCR; laser disc player; television monitor; all completed worksheets.

Teaching Strategy: Using the index volumes to the *Video Encyclopedia*, students will find film clips featuring the people they have selected as twentieth century heroes. They will view the film clips and use worksheet 3.5 to record the information found. Worksheet 3.5 also provides space for students to justify their selections of heroes. The class will discuss the heroes selected, with students defending their selections. If necessary, the class will refine its definition of *hero*.

After all students have viewed their selected film clips, the teacher or librarian will choose a group of students to videotape their selections based on worksheet 3.5 and the written reports.

Teaching Plan IV: Making the Videotape (Worksheet 3.6)

Materials: *The Video Encyclopedia of the 20th Century*: laser discs, reference and index volumes; VCR; laser disc player; video camera; television monitor.

Teaching Strategy: Selected students will work together to make one videotape that includes film clips of each of their heroes. The teacher or librarian will select students to participate in this group based on how well their heroes meet the class's definition of *hero* and the quality of the students' research. These students will work together to view the film clips of each hero that they selected and to decide which clips to include on the tape. Students will copy film clips from the *Video Encyclopedia* onto one videotape. They will view the completed tape and will then write a script to be read as the audio portion of the tape. Students should be provided with instructions for dubbing using available equipment. Worksheet 3.6 will guide students through the process of creating the videotape. The audio script must explain what is happening on the film clip and should synchronize with it. Each student in the group should write the script for their selections using worksheet 3.5 and their written reports. Each of these students will be responsible for reading their script when dubbing.

In addition to the videotape of the heroes, the students who work on this project will be videotaped explaining why they chose the heroes they did.

The completed written reports and videotapes may be added to the library media center collection and used for both social studies and language arts classes.

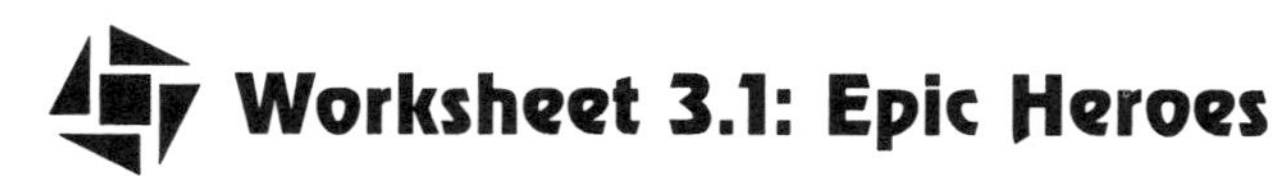

Worksheet 3.1: Epic Heroes

Epic or legendary heroes personify the highest ideals of a nation; and in doing so, they become models for an entire society. The epic hero is courageous and wise, a symbol of all the characteristics that a nation idolizes at a particular period in history. Sometimes epic heroes are based on real people whose feats were so great that stories were told and songs were sung about them. For example, no one is sure if King Arthur or Robin Hood really existed, and if they did how much the stories about them became exaggerated in the telling and retelling.

Select a book to read about epic heroes and answer the following questions.

QUESTIONS

Title: Author:

1. Name of the hero or heroine.
2. In what country did this legendary hero live?
3. What feats make him or her a hero?
4. How would you describe his or her character or personality?
5. What does this tell you about the country in which the hero lived?
6. Do you believe that this person really lived? Why or why not?
7. What personality characteristics do we in this country admire?
8. Can you think of someone famous who has these characteristics?
9. Do you think this person is a hero? Explain.
10. Can you think of a contemporary man or woman who can be compared with the epic hero you read about? Why?

Worksheet 3.2: Defining Hero

Do you have a hero, a famous man or woman you admire and idolize? Someone who has done something so special as to be considered a hero of the twentieth century? Someone who can be compared to an epic hero? We are going to use *The Video Encyclopedia of the 20th Century* to find film clips about twentieth century heroes. But first we must define what we mean when we talk about heroes and decide which feats of courage or special talents should be considered for this project. This worksheet will help you define what is a hero.

QUESTIONS

Defining Hero

1. List several dictionary definitions of *hero*.

2. List the key words common to the definitions.

Role Models

1. List any definitions of *role model* you can find.

2. How do role models differ from heroes?

Questions to Think About

1. Will this project include sports figures and entertainers or only leaders in civil rights, the military, or politics?
2. What kinds of deeds should be considered heroic?

3. Should any deeds not be considered heroic?

4. What famous men and women have characteristics that are not heroic? Name the people and explain.

5. Define *hero* for this project.

(Worksheet 3.2—continued)

TWENTIETH CENTURY HEROES

Following is a list of famous people who appear on the *Video Encyclopedia*. Choose one of these people or use the *Video Encyclopedia* index to find another person to research.

Civil Rights Leaders and Activists

Rosa Parks, Martin Luther King, Jr., Gloria Steinem, Betty Friedan

Sports

Muhammad Ali, Jesse Owens, Roger Bannister, Babe Ruth, Olga Korbut, Dorothy Hamill, Althea Gibson, Billie Jean King

World Leaders and U.S. Presidents

Franklin Delano Roosevelt, Winston Churchill, Mahatma Gandhi, John F. Kennedy, Indira Gandhi, Margaret Thatcher, Golda Meir

Entertainers

Marion Anderson, Leonard Bernstein

Military Leaders

Gen. Dwight D. Eisenhower, Gen. Douglas MacArthur, Olvita Culp Hobby

Scientists and Inventors

Orville Wright and Wilbur Wright, Thomas A. Edison, Jonas Salk, Albert Einstein, Marie Curie, Rosalyn Yalow

Humanitarians

Eleanor Roosevelt, Helen Keller

Aviators

Amelia Earhart, Charles Lindbergh

U.S. Supreme Court Justices

Thurgood Marshall, Sandra Day O'Connor

Worksheet 3.3: Biographies and Biographical Sources

A biography is someone's life story written by another person. A biography tells what the person did during his or her life. Biographers use diaries, letters, newspaper articles, interviews, and anything that has been written about the person to gather information. Information about a person may be found in many places, and very often many sources must be used to get a complete picture of a person's life and accomplishments.

GLOSSARY: PARTS OF A BIOGRAPHY

When you read a biography, check to see whether it includes any of the following elements. A good biography includes at least one.

Author Notes. Tell about the author's qualifications for writing this biography.

Bibliography. A list of books for further reading about the subject. Check this list to find additional material.

Glossary. A small dictionary that defines unfamiliar terms used in the book.

Source Notes. Tell where the author found the information.

GLOSSARY: KINDS OF BIOGRAPHIES

Fictional Biographies. Combine facts and fiction. Although based on real people and events, the author adds conversations and events that might not have happened.

Historical Biographies. Tell about people who lived in the past.

Popular Biographies. Tell about the lives of people in the news.

SOURCES OF BIOGRAPHICAL INFORMATION

Individual Biography

Use the catalog in the school or public library to find a biography of the person you are researching. But don't stop there. One source of information is not enough. Authors see a person's life from various points of view, and it is important to gather information from various authors so that you can draw your own conclusions about the person and his or her achievements. Check to see if the biography you chose includes a bibliography, glossary, or notes.

List the title, author, and publication date for each book you read.

Title:	Title:
Author:	Author:
Date:	Date:

(Worksheet 3.3– continued)

Collective Biography

A collective biography contains many biographies of people who have something in common, for example, United States presidents or inventors or athletes. You will find collective biographies by asking yourself, "Why is this person famous?" and looking up the subject in the catalog. When you find a collective biography on the subject you need, check the table of contents to see if the person you are researching is listed.

List the title, author, and publication date for each collective biography you read.

Title:

Author:

Date:

Title:

Author:

Date:

Biographical Dictionaries

These reference books offer short accounts of the most important facts about many people's lives. Some biographical dictionaries cover only people who are deceased. Some cover people who were alive when the book was written but who may have died since. It is important to check the publication date and to read the preface and the explanatory notes to understand the kinds of information in the volume. Following is a list of some biographical dictionaries found in most libraries. Try to find information about the person you are researching using two of these dictionaries or others available in your library.

Webster's New Biographical Dictionary

Who's Who in American History

Men of Science in America

Who's Who of American Women

Twentieth Century Authors

Women of Achievement

List the title and publication date of the two dictionaries you used.

Title: Date:

Title: Date:

Current Biography

Current Biography, published monthly, contains articles about people currently in the news. These people may be prominent in the arts, science, national and international affairs, or industry. This publication began in 1940, and many libraries have back issues. It is an excellent source, because the biographies are lengthy and offer a great deal of information.

Biography Index

Another good source of biographical information is the *Biography Index*. This tells you where to find biographical information in books and periodicals. If your library has this index, use it to learn where to find information about the person you are researching.

Worksheet 3.4: Taking Notes

As you gather information from the books and periodicals you read, answer the following questions. You will use this information in a written report.

QUESTIONS

1. When was this person born?
2. If dead, when did he or she die?
3. Where was the person born and reared? What is the person's ethnic or racial background?
4. Who had the greatest influence on this person? Describe the way in which the person was influenced.
5. What events influenced this individual's life?
6. Did this person have to overcome hardships? Explain why that effort qualifies the person as a hero.
7. What did this person contribute to society? Are those contributions heroic? Why?
8. Evaluate the contributions and explain how they helped to improve people's lives.
9. List in chronological order the most important events in this person's life.
10. What are the special qualities or characteristics that make you consider this person a hero?
11. Explain how this person meets the definition of hero that we decided to use for this project (see worksheet 3.2).
12. Add any information you think is important.

(Worksheet 3.4—continued)

EPIC VS. REAL HEROES

How do the real-life heroes selected for this project compare with heroes of legend? Is it possible for a real person of recent memory to be as noble and courageous as the heroes of legend? Or are legends embroidered so that the heroes fit the mold that people want to believe it is possible to achieve? Answer the following questions.

QUESTIONS

1. Why is the person you selected famous?

2. What characteristics do we admire in a person in this country?

3. Does the twentieth century hero that you selected meet these criteria? How?

4. Compare the feats performed by this real person with those of the legendary hero you read about.

5. Do you think the acts of the real-life hero were as courageous as those of the epic hero? Why or why not?

6. Can you think of a contemporary hero, other that the one you selected, who might compare with the epic hero? Explain.

Worksheet 3.5: Using the Video Encyclopedia

Use the *Video Encyclopedia* to find information about the person you have selected as your twentieth century hero. View all the film clips you can find. Each clip will give you a different look at the person; after viewing all of the clips, decide which you will use for the video report. Just as a written report does not contain all the information you read in a reference book, your video report will not use all the available film clips. Your teacher or librarian will select those students whose heroes will be used for the videotape.

Use the index volume to the *Video Encyclopedia* to find the person you selected. Use the worksheet to record the following information from the index and reference volumes for each film clip that you find.

Person's name:

Reference number: Laser disc number: Slide/chapter number:

Running time: Video/Audio:

Unit title: Year:

QUESTIONS

Read the reference notes in the reference volume and answer the following questions.

1. What is the person doing on this film clip?
2. Are there any other people on the clip?
3. What is the importance of the film clip?
4. What does this film clip tell you about the person's character or accomplishments?
5. How does the film clip help you better understand the person?
6. Do you think that the class definition of *hero* needs to be changed? If so, rewrite the definition.

Using the class definition of *hero*, the information you gathered from reading the biographies and biographical sources, and the *Video Encyclopedia*, write a report that defends your selection of this person as a twentieth century hero. Write the report on a separate sheet of paper.

Worksheet 3.6: Making the Videotape

This project consists of two parts. In the first part, you will combine film clips from *The Video Encyclopedia of the 20th Century* with an audio script that you write to create a videotape about your heroes. In the second part, you will write a brief explanation of why you chose the hero you did, and you will be videotaped giving that explanation.

SELECTING FILM CLIPS

The *Video Encyclopedia* may include several film clips of some heroes; you will work as a group to choose the ones best suited to this project. The total length of the videotape, with all the film clips, should be no longer than 15-20 minutes.

Following are some criteria for selecting film clips:

- The film clip should clearly indicate why this person is a hero.
- If there are several similar film clips, choose only one.
- Choose film clips that focus on the person; avoid clips in which the person has a secondary role.
- If there is a good picture of the person speaking, use it. But don't use a long speech unless you voice-over part of it.

COPYING FILM CLIPS ONTO VIDEOTAPE

1. Stack the laser discs in the order in which you will record them.
2. Turn on the television monitor, VCR, and laser disc player. Be sure that the television and VCR are on channel 3.
3. Using the laser disc player remote control, press Eject once. Place the first laser disc on the tray.
4. Press Chapter on the laser disc remote control and enter the number of the chapter.
5. Press Search on the laser disc remote control.
6. When the picture appears on the screen, press Record on the VCR. *Do not use the VCR remote control.* Be careful not to record the chapter numbers as they appear on the screen.
7. When the film clip is copied, press pause on the VCR.
8. Repeat this procedure for each film clip you wish to copy. NOTE: It is not necessary to use the Record button on the VCR again. Just press Pause to stop, and press it again to restart recording.
9. When you are done taping, remove the last laser disc. Press Play on the laser disc remote control to close the tray.
10. View each clip to be sure it is complete.

(Worksheet 3.6—continued)

ADDING AUDIO

Using notes, explain what is happening on the video. This should be done for each film clip selected. If the person is speaking on the film clip, you may decide to voice-over what is being said or leave it unchanged.

View the videotape before recording the audio. Follow your teacher or librarian's instructions for audio dubbing. It is very important for the audio to synchronize with the video for the tape to make any sense.

The students whose heroes were selected should be videotaped explaining the project and why they selected these people as their heroes.

After you complete the videotape about heroes, write a brief explanation of why you chose the hero you did. Practice reading the explanation or memorize it. Have a classmate videotape you explaining why this person is your hero.

The New Immigrants: Melting Pot or Gorgeous Mosaic?

Some of the students in my school have recently arrived from Puerto Rico, the Dominican Republic, Ecuador, Colombia, Trinidad, Guyana, Mexico, and Jamaica. Several teachers have recently arrived from Nigeria, The Philippines, and the Caribbean island of Martinique.

Immigration is nothing new. What is new are the countries of origin. Before 1965 most immigrants came from Europe. Although there was hostility to many of the newcomers, they assimilated, and their children and grandchildren became part of American society. During the 1920s a limit was set on the number of immigrants who could enter this country: as a result very few non-Europeans immigrated.

In 1965, when quotas were lifted, a new wave of immigration began, with people coming from Asian and Hispanic countries. These arrivals spawned a wave of racism and an awareness of a growing multicultural population. Many immigrants, although eager to participate in American culture, do not want to give up their native language and customs. This has led to conflict between people who assert that assimilation is necessary to maintain America's melting-pot culture and those who believe that multiculturalism can only enrich American society.

Many Americans are wary of people who look different and whose culture seems alien to that of the European countries from which they came. All too frequently this diversity of culture leads to conflict and misunderstanding. People often have little knowledge of each other's history, religion, and traditions. They are suspicious of what they do not understand and cannot fathom what seems strange and alien to them.

Former New York City mayor David Dinkins called New York a "gorgeous mosaic" because of all the many groups that live side by side, practicing their religions, speaking their native languages, and maintaining customs and cultures of their native lands. However, some people argue that this diversity can only lead to problems; that people must learn new ways in a new country and cannot retain a foreign language and customs if both they and the United States are to succeed. These assimilationists believe that immigrants should learn American customs and English as quickly as possible. On the other side of the argument, multiculturalists feel that assimilation leads to identity loss, that customs should not become homogenized, and that people should retain the language of their forebears even as they learn English.

This chapter focuses on the debate about multiculturalism. It focuses on the cultural diversity of new immigrants, problems they encounter upon arriving in this country, conflicts that occur among various racial and ethnic groups, and what can be done to resolve these conflicts.

The projects in this chapter teach students to look for information in a variety of sources. First, the *Readers' Guide to Periodical Literature* is introduced. Then students are introduced to online searching using a bibliographic database. Students are encouraged to look for information in fiction as well as nonfiction, including biographies. The students engage in a videotaped debate on multiculturalism. Students who do not participate in the debate will judge it. Finally, all students participate in a discussion of the issue. Table 4.1 is a timetable of all the projects in this chapter.

Each group of students will focus on a particular immigrant group. They will use *Readers' Guide to Periodical Literature* and an online bibliographic database, such as WILSONLINE, to learn about the political and economic conditions that may have induced the immigrants to leave their native countries. They will also read fiction and biographies dealing with the immigrant experience. They will research various opinions regarding multicultural society and multicultural education, and they will take part in a videotaped debate on the subject.

Using a bibliographic database, such as WILSONLINE, enables students to locate a broad range of current information outside the school or public library. Online retrieval helps students develop important research skills as they learn to access, search, and evaluate appropriate databases while developing subject bibliographies. Online searching

Table 4.1
Timetable for The New Immigrants

Project	Number of Library Periods	Number of Class Periods
Researching the Topic		
Worksheet 4.1: Using *Readers' Guide to Periodical Literature*	2	2
Worksheet 4.2: Taking Notes		4
Worksheet 4.3: Using WILSONLINE	2 2 (per group)	
The Immigrant Experience		
Worksheet 4.4: Reading About the Immigrant Experience	1	2
The Debate		
Worksheet 4.5: Preparing for the Debate	1 4 (for debaters*)	
Worksheet 4.6: Judging the Debate	2	
Total	8 +2 (per group) +4 (for debaters)	8

*After debaters have been chosen they will use the library to prepare for the debate.

motivates students by the ease of access and because it is fun to use computers. The Boolean search operators *and, not, or* are used for all online searching. Teaching Boolean search strategies will allow students to apply what they learn to other bibliographic databases as well as online encyclopedias, computerized catalogs, and CD-ROM encyclopedias. It will allow students to find more precise information than searching a card catalog ever will.[1] However, because of the cost involved, it is necessary to prepare students carefully before they go online.

Debating promotes cooperation among students who work together toward a goal, using reasoning skills and synthesizing materials from a variety of sources. Debating enhances a competitive spirit while emphasizing fair play, all the while honing oral communication skills. The debate procedures outlined for this project are simplified; the intricacies of the debate will depend on the experience and grade of the debaters or judges.

Notes

1. Ala, Judy, and Kathy Cerabona, "Boolean Searches—A Life Skill," *School Library Journal* (November 1992): 42.

Bibliography

* Denotes entries taken from *Global Beat*, New York Public Library, Office of Young Adult Services (1992).

Branson, Karen. *Streets of Gold.* New York: Putnam, 1981. Immigrant Irish girl.

*Buss, Fran Leeper. *Journey of the Sparrows*. New York: Lodestar Books, 1991. A Salvadoran refugee family tries to adjust to life in Chicago.

*Chin, Frank. *Donald Duk*. Minneapolis: Coffee House Press, 1991. Donald's name doesn't help him avoid trouble.

*Crew, Linda. *Children of the River*. New York: Delacorte Press, 1989. A Cambodian teenager has a hard time fitting in at an Oregon high school.

Gurasich, Marj. *Letters to Oma*. Forth Worth: Texas Christian University Press, 1989. In 1847 a young girl from Germany moves to Texas. In letters to her grandmother, she relates the family's struggles.

Kushner, Donn. *Uncle Jacob's Ghost Story*. New York: Holt, Rinehart, and Winston, 1986. Polish immigrants in New York City.

Lehrman, Robert. *The Store That Mama Built.* New York: Macmillan, 1992. In 1917, Jewish immigrants from Russia help run a family store.

Levine, Ellen. *I Hate English.* New York: Scholastic, 1989. Mei Mei, a young girl from Hong Kong, finds it difficult to learn English.

Levitin, Sonia. *Silver Days.* New York: Atheneum, 1989. A Jewish family escapes from Hitler's Germany.

Mathabane, Mark. *Kaffir Boy in America: An Encounter with Apartheid.* New York: Collier Books, 1990. A young South African man starts a new life in America.

Mayerson, Evelyn Wilde. *The Cat Who Escaped from Steerage.* New York: Scribner, 1990. The experiences of Polish immigrants as they journey to the United States.

Miller-Lachman, Lyn. *Our Family, Our Friends, Our World.* New York: R. R. Bowker, 1992.

Mills, Claudia. *Luisa's American Dream.* New York: Four Winds Press, 1981. A Catholic schoolgirl is embarrassed by her Cuban immigrant parents.

*Paulsen, Gary. *The Crossing.* New York: Orchard Books, 1987. Manuel flees across the Mexican-U.S. border to save his life.

Sandin, Joan. *The Long Way Westward.* New York: Harper & Row, 1989. Swedish immigrants make their way from New York to Minnesota.

——. *The Long Way to a New Land.* New York: Harper & Row, 1986. From Sweden to America in 1868.

*Santiago, Danny. *Famous All Over Town,* New York: New American Library, 1983. A Mexican immigrant's son has trouble fitting in.

Shefelman, Janice J. *A Paradise Called Texas.* Austin: Eakin, 1983. In 1845 Mina and her family leave Germany for Texas.

*Soto, Gary. *Baseball in April and Other Stories,* San Diego: Harcourt Brace Jovanovich, 1990. Adventures in the daily lives of Mexican-American teenagers and children.

*Villasenor, Victor Edmundo. *Macho.* Houston: Arte Publico Press, 1991. Roberto crosses the Mexican-U.S. border to look for fortune for his family in Mexico.

Whelan, Gloria. *Goodbye Vietnam.* New York: Alfred A. Knopf, 1992. A dangerous sea voyage to Hong Kong for a 13-year-old girl escaping the brutal government of Vietnam.

Yee, Paul. *Tales from Gold Mountain.* New York: Macmillan, 1989. Eight original stories based on the history of Chinese immigrants in North America.

Yep, Laurence. *The Star Fisher.* New York: Morrow Junior Books, 1991. A Chinese girl meets both prejudice and friendship in West Virginia in the 1920s.

——. *Mountain Light.* New York: Harper & Row, 1985.

A 19-year-old boy leaves China to seek his fortune in the California gold fields.

Biography

*Ashabranner, Brent. *New Americans.* New York: Dodd, Mead, 1983. Experiences of some recent immigrants and U.S. immigration history.

*Catalano, Grace. *Gloria Estefan.* New York: St. Martin's Press, 1991. Hard work brings Estefan and the Miami Sound Machine to the top in pop, rock, and Latino music.

*Kherdian, David. *The Road from Home: The Story of an Armenian Girl.* New York: Greenwillow Books, 1979. A young girl survives the Turkish massacre of Armenians and reaches the United States at the age of 16.

*Kurelek, William. *They Sought a New World.* Montreal, Plattsburgh, N.Y.: Tundra Books, 1985. In words and pictures, European immigrants describe the challenges they faced coming to the United States and Canada.

*Morey, Janet Nomura, and Wendy Dunn. *Famous Asian Americans.* New York: Cobblehill Books, 1992. Lives of men and women born to immigrant parents.

*Santoli, Al. *New Americans: An Oral History.* New York: Viking, 1988. Thirty immigrants from 16 counties tell why they left their homelands, how they got to America, and what happened after they arrived.

Teaching Plan I: Researching the Topic (Worksheets 4.1, 4.2, and 4.3)

Materials: Class set of instructions for using *Readers' Guide to Periodical Literature*; articles copied from periodicals; access to bibliographic database, such as WILSONLINE; modem; computer; printer.

Teaching Strategy: The classroom teacher will introduce the subject of immigration and multiculturalism, then divide the class into groups. Studying the immigrant experience and understanding the cultural diversity of immigrant groups will give students insight into the issue of multiculturalism. Each group will research a recent immigrant group and the arguments for and against a multicultural society. The teacher will introduce the vocabulary of multiculturalism.

The class set of instructions to the *Readers' Guide to Periodical Literature* (see appendix) will be used to introduce periodical searching. Students will begin their research. Worksheets 4.1 and 4.2 are guides to help students use *Readers' Guide* and take notes to prepare for the debate about multiculturalism.

When students have practiced using *Readers' Guide* and found articles for their research, they will learn to search the bibliographic database WILSONLINE. Instructions for using WILSONLINE appear on worksheet 4.3.

Teaching Plan II: The Immigrant Experience (Worksheet 4.4)

Materials: Bibliography of fiction and biography about the immigrant experience; printouts from students' online searches.

Teaching Strategy: The librarian will introduce students to fiction and biography about the immigrant experience in the United States. Each student will read one novel or biography. Reading stories about immigrant families and their experiences will help youngsters understand the kinds of hardships immigrants have faced and how they have adjusted despite these hardships. A bibliography of such books appears on pages 44-45. Add to it appropriate titles that students found during their online searches.

After students finish their assigned reading, they will discuss the immigrant experience; discussion questions appear on worksheet 4.4. This discussion will lead to further insight into the issue of multiculturalism and make for a better debate.

Teaching Plan III: The Debate (Worksheets 4.5 and 4.6)

Materials: Student research, copies of historical debates found in the library, books on debating techniques, video camera and tape.

Teaching Strategy: After the class has completed its research and has read fiction and biographies dealing with the immigrant experience, the classroom teacher will introduce students to debating and to famous historical debates. An excellent source for a discussion of historical debates appears in *Cobblestone: The History Magazine for Young People* (January 1987, vol. 8, no. 1). The classroom teacher will distribute the worksheets to the entire class, and will select students to participate in the debate based on the quality of the students' research. The debate requires four students for the negative team and four for the affirmative. Worksheet 4.5 is an introduction to debate language and procedure. Worksheet 4.6 is a form to use for judging. All students who do not take part in the debate will act as judges. A discussion of the issues will follow. The debate and discussion should be videotaped and presented to other classes as an introduction to the issue of multiculturalism and to debating.

One book that may help students learn to debate is *How to Debate* by Robert E. Dunbar (Franklin Watts, 1987).

Worksheet 4.1: Using the Readers' Guide to Periodical Literature

Do you believe that America should be a melting pot in which people assimilate quickly and give up their native language and customs? Or do you see the value in a "gorgeous mosaic," a country made up of many languages and customs, in which people respect each other while learning to live together in harmony?

Some of the native countries of recent immigrants are Cambodia, Laos, Vietnam, China, Korea, Thailand, the Philippines, Mexico, Puerto Rico, the Dominican Republic, Cuba, Guyana, Guatemala, and Russia. Each group of students will choose one country to research. Begin to think about how you feel about this issue.

You will be doing research using *Readers' Guide to Periodical Literature* to prepare for a debate on the issue of a multicultural society. Each student will take part in the debate as a debater or a judge. A debate is a way of discussing an issue where the question being discussed is open to different opinions and interpretations. A debate always involves a judge or moderator who listens to arguments from both sides and then decides which side has presented the stronger arguments in defense of his or her position. Your research will provide you with information for the debate.

IMPORTANT TERMS

Use a dictionary to find definitions for each of the following terms.

Assimilate

Bilingualism

Ethnocentrism

Melting Pot

Mosaic

Multicultural

Nativist

READERS' GUIDE TO PERIODICAL LITERATURE

Readers' Guide is an index to popular magazines. The up-to-date information found in magazines often is not available in books because books take longer to publish than magazines. Some smaller libraries use the *Abridged Readers' Guide*, which indexes fewer magazines but includes enough to use for this project. Articles are indexed by the subject of the article and sometimes the author. The *Readers' Guide* gives a citation for the article, not the article itself.

In the front of the *Readers' Guide*, you will find a list of magazines that are indexed as well as a list of the abbreviations used in the citations. The citation includes

- the name of the magazine in which the article was printed;
- the author and title of the article;
- the volume and issue numbers, page numbers, and date of publication;

(Worksheet 4.1—continued)

- subject heading and subheading: a subject heading is sometimes divided into smaller topics. These are found in bold letters in the center of the column. They refer you to additional articles.
- cross references: see also references refer you to additional articles. *See* references refer you to the subject heading used in the *Readers' Guide*.

List the subjects you are looking for.

Use the dictionary or thesaurus to find synonyms for these subjects.

Find at least three citations that have those subject headings. Use a separate sheet of paper for each citation, and list the following:

Subject:

Subheading (if any):

Cross references (if any):

Title of article:

Author:

Name of magazine:

Publication date: Volume, issue, and page numbers:

Obtain the issues of the magazines in your school or public library or through interlibrary loan. Copy the articles to use for your research.

Worksheet 4.2: Taking Notes

To prepare for a debate, you will take notes from the articles you found using the *Readers' Guide to Periodical Literature*. The proposition of the debate is: "A Multicultural Society Benefits the United States." During the debate, arguments and evidence will be presented for and against that proposition. The winner of the debate will be determined by the strength of the evidence presented. Take notes carefully to ensure that all evidence is accurately recorded. The teacher will choose the students to take part in the debate on the basis of their notes. All other students will be judges. Complete each of the following steps to prepare for the debate.

1. Read each article carefully.
2. Record your notes and the reasons for or against the proposition. These reasons are called arguments. Record each argument, pro or con, on a separate sheet of paper. As you read each article, add facts and opinions to help prove each argument. This is your evidence. You will need both pro and con arguments for the debate.
3. Reread the articles. *In your own words* record all the information you need for the debate. If you have a problem putting the information in your own words, underline the key or most important words as you reread the articles. Then use these words in your own sentences. *Don't let your opinions get in the way of recording the facts.*
4. Include quotations from authorities or organizations that can be used during the debate. These will lend weight to your argument. Don't put quotations in your own words. *Copy them exactly.* Include the name of the person quoted and when and where the quote was made, if that information is available.

ARGUMENTS

Pro or con argument:

Evidence from source 1:

Quotation:

Source of quotation:

Notes:

Evidence from source 2:

Quotation 2:

Source 2:

Notes:

Use the back of this worksheet and additional sheets of paper if you find additional sources of evidence for this argument. Complete the following fact sheet. If your answers here provide evidence for the debate, add the information.

(Worksheet 4.2—continued)

FACT SHEET

Name of immigrant group:

Country of origin of immigrant group:

Continent on which the country is located:

Major religion of immigrant group:

Race of immigrant group:

Language of immigrant group:

Educational level of immigrants:

Economic conditions of the country of origin:

Form of government:

Political conditions that may have caused immigrants to leave country:

Other possible reasons for these immigrants to leave their native country (for example, religious discrimination):

Where have large numbers of the immigrants settled? Do they tend to settle in large cities or smaller communities?

What problems have they encountered in the United States?

Describe ways in which they have or have not assimilated.

Have these immigrants made important contributions to the United States? In what ways? Cite evidence.

Quotations about the contributions of the immigrant group:

Source of quotations:

What information that you gathered on the fact sheet can be used as evidence for or against multiculturalism?

Worksheet 4.3: Using WILSONLINE

Readers' Guide pointed you to recent articles about the subject you are researching. An online database, such as WILSONLINE, provides information that is more frequently updated and easier to use than a print index. It leads you to more information through the use of additional Wilson indexes. However online searching is expensive. You must prepare your research strategy carefully before you go online to avoid wasting money.

GLOSSARY: ONLINE TERMS

Bibliographic database. A database of citations, or information about documents. This information usually includes title; author; name of the periodical with volume, issue, and page numbers, if applicable; subject headings; source; and sometimes a short summary of the contents of the document or article. WILSONLINE is a bibliographic database.

Boolean operators. *See* **Logical operators**.

Citation. Basic information that will help you find an article or document. This information usually includes title; author; and name of the periodical with volume, issue, and page numbers, if applicable. What additional information do the citations in *Readers' Guide* provide?

Communications software. Software that allows you to use your computer to send and receive information over telephone lines. Can you name the communications software used in your library media center?

Database. A collection of related records, also called a file.

Dedicated telephone line. A telephone line used only for telecommunications.

File. *See* **Database**.

Index. An alphabetical listing of subjects. *Readers' Guide* is an index to magazine articles.

Key words. The most important words you use in your search.

Logical operators. Words used to create statements to narrow or broaden a search. You will use three logical operators: *and, or, not*. Note the differences among the following:

Immigration
Immigration *AND* Asians
Immigration *NOT* Asians
Immigration *OR* Citizenship

What information will you retrieve using each of these statements? How does the information you will receive from each search statement differ?

Mnemonic. Assisting or intended to assist memory; a memory aid.

Modem. A device used to transmit data among computers over telephone lines.

Online. Connected to and exchanging information with another computer using telephone lines.

Search strategy. A plan for searching for and retrieving information. When using an online bibliographic database, it is important to plan your search before you go online, because online searching is expensive.

(Worksheet 4.3—continued)

SEARCH STRATEGY

1. List the most meaningful or important words in your notes. These are the key words that you will use when you search the database.

Combine the key words using the logical operators *and, not, or*. Use as many combinations as you can. Some combinations will be your search statements when you go online. Example: Immigration AND Education.

_______________ AND _______________
_______________ NOT _______________
_______________ OR _______________

3. List the search statements, with the one that you think will produce the most citations first. You may not need all of the search statements, but be prepared before going online.

 Search 1:

 Search 2:

 Search 3:

 Search 4:

 Search 5:

4. The abbreviations or mnemonics in parentheses are used to get into the file when you go online. Following is a list of some of the files available on WILSONLINE. List the databases or files you will search.

Biography Index (BIO). Includes information about both individual and collective biographies.

Book Review Digest (BRD). Excerpts of reviews for current fiction and nonfiction.

Cumulative Book Index (CBI). Index to information about English language books.

Readers' Guide to Periodical Literature (RDG). Index to popular magazines.

Social Science Index (SSI). All areas of social science, including ethnic studies, sociology, minority studies, and economics.

5. You are ready to go online. Have your file mnemonics and search statements ready. Logon procedures differ among communications programs. You librarian will give you the instructions for logon and logoff.

6. During your online search, save your citations to a floppy disk or hard drive. Print a copy off-line. This bibliography will be saved for use by other classes.

(Worksheet 4.3—continued)

7. Obtain the articles in your bibliography from your school or public libraries or through interlibrary loan.

8. Add to the arguments and evidence you already have. Begin a new sheet of paper for each additional argument you find. Remember to include quotations and the name of the person you are quoting.

9. Compare *Readers' Guide* and WILSONLINE. Which gave you the most information? Which was easier to use? Why?

Worksheet 4.4: Reading About the Immigrant Experience

After reading a book about the immigrant experience, answer the following questions.

Title:

Author:

Publisher: Year:

QUESTIONS

1. Who is the protagonist?
2. From what country did he or she emigrate?
3. In what year did he or she arrive in this country?
4. What is the setting?
5. Describe some of the other characters in the book.
6. Is this book based on the author's own experiences?
7. Why did the protagonist immigrate?
8. If the book describes the trip to another country, tell us about it.
9. What hardships did the protagonist face after immigrating?
10. How did he or she overcome these hardships?
11. Did the protagonist integrate successfully into his or her new society?
12. Did the protagonist have to give up cultural heritage or language to assimilate? Explain.
13. Did this book affect how you feel about immigration or a multicultural society? Explain.
14. Do you believe a country is enriched by multiculturalism? Explain.
15. Do you believe there is ever an advantage to a country being monocultural? Explain.

Worksheet 4.5: Preparing for the Debate

You have read about famous historical debates and researched immigration and multiculturalism in preparation for a debate. This worksheet will introduce you to the procedure to be followed during the debate.

PREPARATION

The proposition of this debate is "Resolved: A Multicultural Society Is Beneficial to America."

All arguments for and against the proposition have been researched. You have taken notes from many sources, and gathered evidence and arguments both for and against the proposition. Now you are ready to use this research for the debate. Your teacher will select eight students for the debate, four for each team.

STRUCTURE OF THE DEBATE

Each team consists of four members. The affirmative team includes three affirmative speakers and one affirmative rebuttalist. The negative team includes three negative speakers and one negative rebuttalist.

The order of the speakers is as follows. (The time allocations indicated are suggestions. The teacher and class should determine the time limits before the debate begins.)

First Affirmative Case Speakers

The affirmative team speaks first. The affirmative position is divided between the first two speakers, who have two minutes each to present their case (four minutes total).

First Negative Case Speakers

The negative team responds. The negative position is divided between two speakers, who have two minutes each to refute the affirmative arguments (four minutes total).

Third Affirmative Speaker

This speaker extends and concludes the affirmative team's position with additional evidence and refutes the arguments presented by the negative team (two minutes).

Third Negative Speaker

This speaker extends and concludes the negative team's position with additional evidence and refutes the arguments presented by the third affirmative speaker (two minutes).

Negative Rebuttalist

The negative rebuttalist summarizes and strengthens the arguments that have been presented by the negative team. The negative rebuttalist does not present any new evidence (three minutes).

Affirmative Rebuttalist

The affirmative rebuttalist summarizes the affirmative team's position and may present new evidence to rebut a new negative argument that was presented by the third negative speaker (three minutes).

(Worksheet 4.5—continued)

PREPARATION TIME

Preparation time is allowed between each presentation *except between the first two speakers*. Before each presentation the team should ask for prep time, if the team members feel they need it. A limit on the total amount of preparation time each team may use should be set.

TIMEKEEPER

The teacher will appoint one student to act as timekeeper and moderator. The timekeeper will announce the time limits before the debate begins and will make sure that all participants adhere to the limits. When time runs out the timekeeper will call out "Time" but will allow the speaker to complete his or her sentence.

The timekeeper will keep track of discussion time and preparation time to be sure that each team does not exceed the limits.

PRESENTATIONS

To present an effective case, the first two team members on both the affirmative and negative teams should include in their presentations an introduction to the subject, evidence with quotations from experts, definitions of key words used in the proposition, a defense of the team's position, and a clarification of the issues. The first two speakers for the negative team also must refute the affirmative team's arguments.

The third speaker for each team concludes the team's argument and presents more in-depth evidence to support it. The rebuttalist for each team summarizes the team's position, indicating why its arguments are superior.

RULES

All debates have rules. It is important to establish rules before the debate begins and to be sure that everyone understands them. The class should brainstorm and select the rules together. Following are a few sample rules.

Note passing will be permitted at all times during the debate.

Debaters will talk to each other only during preparation time.

Prepared notes may be referred to but may not be read.

Time allocations for speakers and preparation time for teams should be decided before the debate begins. Every discussion among team members is deducted from the total preparation time allowed.

Worksheet 4.6: Judging the Debate

All class members who are not on the debate teams will act as judges. Because all students researched the topic, everyone should be familiar with the arguments and evidence, both pro and con. Do not let your opinion influence your decision as to the winner of the debate. Winners should be judged on which team has the better arguments and is better prepared. A good debate is a battle of ideas; there should be conflict backed up by evidence, with each team ready to refute the other.

CRITERIA FOR JUDGING

First Affirmative and Negative Cases

Did the first two speakers introduce and clearly present the main issue? Were key words from the proposition well defined? Were the arguments developed in a logical way? Was evidence presented with quotations from experts? Did the negative team speakers adapt their arguments to refute the affirmative team's case?

Second Affirmative and Negative Cases

Did the third speaker complete the team's case by presenting new in-depth evidence? Did the speaker refute the other team's arguments?

Rebuttals

Did students convincingly challenge and rebut opposing arguments? Were errors in one team's evidence pointed out by the other team? Did a team fail to disprove an argument by the opposing team where it could have done so? Was the team's case effectively summarized?

Overall Presentation

Did students speak clearly, convincingly, and slowly enough to be understood? Was the evidence presented in a way that held the audience's interest? If listeners knew nothing about the subject, could they have understood both the pro and con arguments well enough to come to a conclusion about the proposition? Were the cases and rebuttals completed in the time allotted?

BALLOT

Score each category from 1 to 5, with 5 the highest score possible and 1 the lowest. Do not allow your opinions or friendships to influence your judgment! Speakers should be rated only on their presentations within each category.

1. **First two affirmative speakers**
   Introduction (statement of support) __________
   Evidence cited to support proposition __________
   Key terms defined __________
   Overall presentation __________

   Total __________

(Worksheet 4.6—continued)

2. **First two negative speakers**
   Introduction (statement of nonsupport) __________
   Key words defined __________
   Evidence cited for nonsupport __________
   Refuted affirmative arguments __________
   Overall presentation

   Total __________

3. **Third affirmative speaker**
   Extended affirmative case __________
   Completed affirmative case __________
   Refuted the negative position __________
   Overall presentation __________

   Total __________

4. **Third negative speaker**
   Extended the negative case __________
   Completed the negative case __________
   Refuted the affirmative position __________
   Overall presentation __________

   Total __________

5. **Negative rebuttal**
   Reviewed negative case __________
   Gave reasons negative case holds __________
   Gave reasons affirmative case fails __________
   Summation __________
   Overall presentation __________

   Total __________

6. **Affirmative rebuttal**
   Reviewed affirmative case __________
   Gave reasons affirmative case holds __________
   Gave reasons negative case fails __________
   Summation __________
   Overall presentation __________

   Total __________

7. **Total Score**
   Affirmative team __________
   Negative team __________

Name of Judge:

(Worksheet 4.6—continued)

CLASS DISCUSSION

1. Did the debate make you change your mind about the value of multiculturalism?

2. Were any important issues not presented?

3. What were they?

4. How do you feel about a multicultural society? Give reasons for your opinions.

5. Did you think the scoring of the debate was fair?

6. Do you agree with the class's judgment? Why or why not?

The debate and following discussion should be videotaped for presentation at parent association meetings and district office workshops and to other classes.

Terrorism: A Fact of Life for the 1990s

Terrorism is "the sustained, clandestine use of violence—murder, kidnapping, hijacking, bombings—to achieve a political purpose."[1] Terrorism almost always involves acts of violence against civilians with the intent to influence the opinions of the populace or the actions of its leaders. Terrorism is a fact of modern life.

The projects in this chapter, designed for advanced eighth and ninth graders, investigate terrorism from the viewpoints of terrorists, hostages, negotiators, the media, and government officials. Students will research the history of terrorism and terrorist groups for information to be used in writing a play. Table 5.1 is a time line of the three projects included in this chapter.

In addition to searching the catalogs in the school and local public libraries, students will conduct online searches of at least one public access catalog. This will show them the extensive resources available from many different sources through interlibrary loan. In New York City, for example, school libraries have access to the Metropolitan Inter-Library Cooperative System (MILCS) online catalog; this collection of catalogs makes the vast holdings of many libraries available to a small school library. The MILCS catalog includes the holdings of hundreds of libraries within the New York City metropolitan area and thus allows students to research a subject, such as terrorism, for which our collection is very limited. When we searched the card catalog in our school library we found nothing. A search of the neighborhood public library produced slightly better results. Our next try was the MILCS online catalog, where we were able to find 262 entries. We certainly did not need all 262, but the wider search helped us find the information we did need. Using only the school library would have limited our search to encyclopedia articles. Outside the school we found material suitable for advanced students but not for the general school population. The school's very limited budget precludes collecting such materials. The online catalog solves the problem of helping a small number of students without penalizing the greater number.

One study conducted in North Carolina found that many benefits accrued to students from online catalog searching. The benefits include not only improved search skills but also a greater understanding of the research process because of the logic involved in the online search. In addition, the wide range of resources available impressed upon students the need to clearly understand the appropriateness of available resources and the need to weed out unsuitable sources. In learning to judge the appropriateness of a source, students applied the higher-order thinking skills of analysis and synthesis.[2]

Students will begin their research in groups using Research Writer software. This program begins with a skyjacking simulation and goes on to provide an excellent introduction to the library research process. Students take notes on the computer and print them throughout the program; they also may find articles about terrorism within the program. The articles are difficult to read, and many of the research strategies may be too difficult even for advanced middle school students. However, the program is so comprehensive and the teacher's guide offers so many research ideas that it is worthwhile for teachers to explore it to determine how much of it their students can absorb.

Students will use what they have learned through research to write a class play about an act of terrorism as seen by several of the key people involved. They will learn about the parts of plays, do improvisations, and understand the differences between writing scripts and short stories. These projects should help students understand how a person's role in an event biases the individual's view of it. Students who are not involved in producing the play will act as evaluators and observers.

Notes

1. Charles Maechling, Jr., "Terrorism," *The Online Edition of Grolier's Academic American Encyclopedia*, Danbury, CT: Grolier's Electronic Publishing, 1991.

2. Margaret H. Bingham, "Results of Two Studies on the Benefits and Pitfalls of Technology-Based Information Accessing," *T.H.E. Journal* 20 (November 1992): 88-92.

Table 5.1
Timetable for Terrorism

Project	Number of Library Periods	Number of Class Periods
Researching Terrorism		
Worksheet 5.1: Using Research Writer	1 4 (per group)	2
Worksheet 5.2: Searching Library Catalogs	2 4 (per group)	
Writing the Play		
Worksheet 5.3: Writing the Play		6
Total	3 +8 (per group)	8

Teaching Plan I: Researching Terrorism (Worksheets 5.1 and 5.2)

Materials: Research Writer software, computer, printer, and access to an online catalog.

Teaching Strategy: Students will be introduced to the topic of terrorism as part of a social studies curriculum that deals with the problems of modern society or as part of the communication arts curriculum. This introduction should include definitions, a historic perspective, and an introduction to various groups presently involved in terrorist activities. After this introduction students will use Research Writer. This software program begins with a simulation of a skyjacking. The simulation introduces the many people who are involved in or affected by a terrorist act and shows how each person sees the act from different points of view. Students will prepare for writing a play by closely observing all the participants in the skyjacking event. Students should be encouraged to make notes to be reviewed before writing the play.

Students will also use Research Writer to learn about research procedures. The program includes many articles that may be used, and it introduces many research procedures. Some of these articles and procedures may be too advanced for this age group. Students will need to use the school and local public libraries' catalogs to find information they can understand. (The teacher and librarian, having previewed the program, will direct students to the parts that they can use.) The software is menu-driven and is both fun and valuable, even if many of the articles and research methods are not used.

Students will use Research Writer in groups. Following work with Research Writer they will search the school library catalog. Then they will use a public library catalog and an online catalog, comparing the kinds and number of research sources available. Instructions for using the online catalog and printed copies of the help screens should be distributed to each group. Because the online search will yield a large volume of material, students will need help to learn how to make judgments about the number and kinds of resources they need for this project. Students will work in groups to use the online catalog.

Each student will write a report about terrorism, explaining the motivation and roles of the people involved. These reports should include information about terrorist groups and acts of terrorism. The reports will be used in writing a play. Students with similar interests should be grouped for playwriting.

Teaching Plan II: Writing the Play (Worksheet 5.3)

Materials: Completed reports on terrorism, computer, word processing software.

Teaching Strategy: The teacher will group students according to the topics they researched. Students will use their completed reports (worksheets 5.1 and 5.2) as a basis for writing the play. The students will understand the differences between writing a play and writing a story, and they will practice listening to dialogue. The class will read some plays in class before they begin writing. Improvisations will be used to encourage students to observe body language and to listen carefully to spoken language. The entire class will take part in writing the class play.

Each group of students will write about one character and will depict the terrorist act from that person's point of view. After each group has written about a character, the class will work together to fit all the pieces into one play. A format for playwriting is included. Writing may be done individually or in groups.

Each student will receive a copy of the completed script. Students who are not actors will participate as stage managers, directors, prompters, or in other off-stage roles. All other students will judge whether the play depicts terrorism as their research indicated it should.

Worksheet 5.1: Using Research Writer

Definitions of terrorism used by the United States government stress the use of violence to coerce or intimidate civilians with the intent to affect government policy. Your class is going to research terrorism. After the research is completed you will write a play based on what you have learned. The play will simulate a terrorist act from the points of view of the people involved in the act.

To begin this project you will use a computer program called Research Writer. The program begins with a simulation of a skyjacking. Next are interviews with people involved with terrorism in many different capacities. The program goes on to show you how to use a library and do research, gathering materials for a research report on terrorism. You may take notes and save them throughout the program. Remember, you will be using this information to write a class play about terrorism, so you will need information that gives you the points of view of several participants.

QUESTIONS: HIJACKING OF FLIGHT 102

Watch the hijacking depicted on the disk. Use the Notes menu to make notes about the event.

1. List and describe the people depicted in the hijacking.

   a.

   b.

   c.

   d.

   e.

2. Describe your attitude toward each of these people.

Interviews

Read the computer directions carefully and print all screens that you will need for further review. Then read the interviews with the hostage negotiator and the president of Newsline Cable and answer the following questions.

Hostage negotiator

1. What personal qualities does it take to be a hostage negotiator?

President, Newsline Cable, Inc.

1. Which do you believe is more important, the public's right to know or the safety of the hostages? Explain.

2. Do you believe that the media helps to create hostage situations? Explain.

(Worksheet 5.1—continued)

3. Read three other interviews and take notes. In the spaces provided below, describe the characteristics of terrorism from each person's point of view.

   a. First person interviewed:

   b. Second person interviewed:

   c. Third person interviewed:

LIBRARY

Take the Research Writer simulated library tour, visiting each part of the library. Print the screens that you think you will need for future reference. Perform the following activities.

1. Name three indexes mentioned in the program.

   a.

   b.

   c.

2. Name three ways of searching in the library catalog.

   a.

   b.

   c.

3. Name two government publications said to be useful in researching terrorism.

   a.

   b.

DEVELOPING THE RESEARCH QUESTION

In the Research Writer library section, read about developing research questions. Start to think about your research questions. Because you are writing a play, you may want your research to focus on an individual character involved in a terrorist act. Another approach would be to focus on terrorist groups or on the media. Answer the following questions to help you determine what your research will target.

1. Which character in the skyjacking interests you the most?
2. What motivates this person to act?
3. What effect does the hijacking have on the involved individuals after the hijacking is over?

(Worksheet 5.1—continued)

4. What is the purpose of terrorism?
5. What are some characteristics of terrorists?
6. What are some methods of terrorism?
7. Do you believe that all political acts of violence are terrorism?
8. What is the difference between a terrorist and a freedom fighter?
9. Why does terrorism seem to be on the rise in modern society?
10. What motivates terrorists?
11. In your opinion does the media help terrorists?
12. Is terrorism ever justified?

Select your research focus, narrow your subject, and structure your research question.
Research question:

READING AND WRITING CENTER

Read the tutorials your teacher chooses for you. Continue the program following your teacher's instructions.

Worksheet 5.2: Searching Library Catalogs

For this activity we will use and compare various library catalogs to find material for your research. All library catalogs, whether a card catalog, book catalog, or an online catalog, may be searched by subject, author, and title.

First, write your research question. Copy it from worksheet 5.1.

Research question:

Use the catalog in your school library to find the subject *terrorism*. How many books on this subject are available? Search the catalog of your nearest public library. How many books are available there?

USING A CATALOG CARD

Look at the sample catalog card and fill in the blanks following it.

303.6
C TERRORISM

Coker, Christopher

Terrorism

1986

32 pp.

Author:

Title:

Call number:

Year of publication:

Is this a subject, author, or title card?

USING A BOOK CATALOG

Book catalogs have replaced card catalogs in many libraries. There are separate volumes for subjects, names or authors, and titles.

(Worksheet 5.2—continued)

TERRORISM
Goode, Stephen. *Guerrilla Warfare and Terrorism.* New York, ©1977, 152p. (355.02G)

Author:

Title:

Publication date: Place of publication:

Call number:

Is this sample entry from the subject, name, or title volume?

USING AN ONLINE CATALOG

Searching an online catalog gives you access to material from a vast number of libraries. As part of searching an online catalog, you will locate the library in which the material is found. Then your librarian will get the material you need through interlibrary loan. Because the keystrokes used in catalog searching may differ from catalog to catalog, be sure to read the instructions for the online catalog you use.

Online catalogs are searched by subject, author, or title. Some catalogs offer additional ways to search, such as by media or through cross-references.

1. List three subject headings that will give you the information you need for your research.
   a.
   b.
   c.
2. Search the catalog for those three subjects. How many titles did you find?

Read through each list of titles and select three that will give you the information you need for your research. For each title you select, find the full citation and the location of the library that has the book. Ask the librarian to obtain the books through interlibrary loan. Use the following forms to record the information you need.

First Book

Title:

Author:

Publisher:

Date of publication:

ISBN number:

Location:

(Worksheet 5.2—continued)

Second Book

Title:

Author:

Publisher:

Date of publication:

ISBN number:

Location:

Third book

Title:

Author:

Publisher:

Date of publication:

ISBN number:

Location:

Begin a new search using the media, cross-reference, or other available option. Choose three more materials and ask your librarian to obtain them for you.

PRIMARY AND SECONDARY SOURCES

Primary sources are original documents and firsthand reports of an event as told by a participant from that person's point of view.

1. Name some places where you might find primary sources.
2. How do you know a primary source when you see one?

Secondary sources are based on primary sources and may be used to influence an audience. Indicate which of the following are primary and which are secondary sources of information.

3. A newspaper account of a terrorist act as reported by a witness on the scene when the bomb went off.
4. A newspaper interview with the terrorist who set the bomb.
5. A newspaper editorial about terrorism based on the writer's opinion.

You will write a play in which the people involved in a terrorist act tell about the event from their points of view. Some of these accounts will be primary sources, but as you will see the people will have very different things to say about the event. When you do your research, be careful to note whether you are using primary or secondary sources.

Worksheet 5.3: Writing the Play

The reports that you wrote on terrorism will be used to write a play. The play will depict an act of terrorism as described by several different people who were involved in it.

A play does not tell what happens, it shows the action. A play is about someone who wants something very badly but must overcome obstacles to get it. Without a conflict you do not have a play. A play takes place in the present tense, although the characters all have histories, and you must find a way to tell your audience about the events that led up to the play's present.

Don't have your characters just talk about the terrorist experience; make your play dramatic, full of suspense and conflict.

GLOSSARY: PARTS OF A PLAY

Characters. Persons or actors in a play. There should be a central character who creates the conflict or wants something very badly and opposing characters who don't want him or her to have it.

Climax. The high point or most dramatic moment.

Complication. Something that delays the resolution or heightens the conflict, making for drama and suspense.

Conflict. The conflict or struggle among the characters.

Crisis. The major turning point in the play or the peak of the conflict.

Exposition. Lets the audience know what has led to the conflict, or what happened before the play began. You must do this without using a narrator. In your play, the exposition will include the history of the terrorist group.

Resolution. The settling of the conflict; the protagonist or the opposition succeeds. The resolution comes after the climax and ties everything together.

Setting. Where the play takes place.

IMPROVISATIONS

Before you begin to write your play, it is a good idea to try some improvisations so you can see and understand what makes a good drama.

In small groups, take turns practicing improvising before the class. Try the following:

Everyday school situations.

A short story. Don't use a narrator, use dialogue from the story.

A fairy tale.

Other situations with strong conflicts.

Observe your classmates and take notes. Describe the conflict, speech, facial expression, and body language. After each improvisation discuss how the scene could be improved and repeat it.

(Worksheet 5.3—continued)

WRITING THE PLAY

Break into groups depending on which character you are writing about. Discuss your research with the other students in the group. Before you begin to write the play discuss the following questions with the group to help you understand your character's behavior and motivation.

Use this worksheet to take notes during the discussion. Use an additional worksheet for the final copy.

QUESTIONS

1. Name of character
2. Describe the character's physical appearance.
3. How is he or she dressed?
4. Where does the character live?
5. What does he or she do for a living?
6. What kind of body language and facial expressions will help us understand your character?
7. Write an autobiography in which the character tells about his or her job, family, hobbies, schooling, physical appearance, beliefs, and interests. Use another sheet of paper if you need it.
8. Will your character talk about or to family members in the play? If so, describe how the character feels about them.
9. Add any information from the research that is important to understanding the character's motivation and behavior.

After each group has written about a character, the entire class will work to fit the pieces together.

10. Who is the central character?
11. Who are the opposing characters?
12. What emotions describe how the characters feel about each other?
13. Which characters like or dislike each other? (Being on the same side doesn't mean they will like each other.)

(Worksheet 5.3—continued)

14. What is the conflict or struggle among the characters? You know all about your character's background and personality. The conflict must be believable. How would a person like your character behave in this situation?

15. What will happen during the climax or most dramatic moment of the play? Which characters will be involved in the climax?

16. After the climax comes the resolution. How is the conflict resolved? What will happen to the characters after the play?

17. What props do you need?

18. Who is assigned to getting them?

FORMAT TO USE WHEN WRITING THE PLAY

Title:
Characters:

Scene 1: (setting) (Write down the characters who appear in this scene and describe what they are doing.)

CHARACTER 1
Character 1: (stage directions)
Dialogue:

CHARACTER 2
Character 2: (stage directions)
Dialogue:

ADDITIONAL CHARACTERS
Repeat for each scene. Follow your teacher's directions for writing individually or in groups.

RESOURCES

If you need help writing the play, consult these books:

Polsky, Milton E. *You Can Write a Play*. New York: Rosen, 1983.

Sklar, Daniel J. *Playmaking: Children Writing and Performing Their Own Plays*. New York: Teachers and Writers Collaborative, 1991.

A Question of Survival: Human Behavior and the Environment

Some seventh graders in my school were researching animal versus human rights. These New York City children, familiar only with zoo animals and house pets, opted without hesitation for the animals. In their eyes human needs took a back seat. As far as they were concerned, it was all quite simple: Humans have the power to destroy, but it is unfair to use this power against animals. It is the role of humans to care for animals, not destroy them. I was gratified but surprised that all took such a vehement stand. I posed all kinds of hypothetical questions: What if land was needed for new homes? What if they were cold and needed animal skins to keep warm? What if they were hungry and needed food? Nothing could change their minds.

According to a recent poll, most Americans are very concerned about the environment.[1] They strongly feel that too little is being done to protect it and that greater efforts are needed to fight pollution and to protect natural areas and wildlife. Those polled indicated that they would make sacrifices toward this end, but 61 percent opposed raising taxes specifically for this purpose.

Students must recognize that they are part of an ecological system that is interdependent and that the destruction of any one part of that system affects everyone, both now and in the future. However, they also must understand how difficult it is for people to change a way of life and how unfair it is to ask people to change their way of life when we may be unwilling to change ours. This chapter focuses on the effects of human behavior on the environment and the consequences of this behavior. It also focuses on the reluctance of people to change their habits even when they know they should. Youngsters must understand environmental issues and the implications of their personal actions. However, they also must understand the cultural values and economics that may be involved and the difficulty of imposing change.

The projects in this chapter make use of two electronic tools: CD-ROM and HyperCard. HyperCard structures information to link text, graphics, sound, and animation. A user can leap from one type of information to another by clicking on buttons. Students will use a commercial HyperCard product for research and then create their own HyperCard stack. (Earthquest Explores Ecology is the learning software and HyperCard the authoring program used in this discussion, but other programs may be substituted.)

In addition to using electronic sources available in the school, students will extend their research by writing to agencies for information and by surveying members of the community. Table 6.1 is a timetable of the projects in this chapter.

Small groups will take turns using the *New Grolier Multimedia Encyclopedia* on CD-ROM; they also will investigate print sources. The *New Grolier Multimedia Encyclopedia* stores all 21 volumes of the *Academic American Encyclopedia* on one disc. Using the electronic encyclopedia beats the tedium and time consumed in doing research in print resources. When they use print encyclopedias, students can spend so much time looking for the information they need that by the time they find it they lack the energy to finish the project. This is especially true in middle schools, where students are easily frustrated: they want results and they want them fast. When students use a print encyclopedia they first must search the index volume and then refer to the volume in which the information appears. Cross-references can take them to several additional volumes. Using an electronic encyclopedia the search starts by clicking the proper menu. The text appears in seconds with cross-references, outline, bibliography, graphics, and sound. Students can save the needed information on the disk, add notes, and print it at a later time.

One of the drawbacks to the *New Grolier Multimedia Encyclopedia* is that the *Academic American Encyclopedia* is somewhat difficult for some students. In addition, if the library has only one computer that can be used to work with the encyclopedia, then only a small group of students can use it at any one time. These disadvantages can be overcome with careful planning.

Table 6.1

Timetable for A Question of Survival

Project	Number of Library Periods	Number of Class Periods
Planning the Research		
Worksheet 6.1: Planning a Research Project	2	2
Worksheet 6.2: Using the *New Grolier Multimedia Encyclopedia*	2 (per group)	
Worksheet 6.3: Electronic Encyclopedia Activity Sheet	2 (per group)	
The Community and the Environment		
Worksheet 6.4: Community Survey: The Environment		2
Worksheet 6.5: Analyzing the Survey Results		2
HyperCard		
Worksheet 6.6: Earthquest Explores Ecology	2 (per group)	
Worksheet 6.7: Working with HyperCard	4 (per group)	4
Total	2 +10 (per group)	10

The first project involves selecting a research topic and planning the research strategy in preparation for the use of the CD-ROM encyclopedia. Students will also write to agencies and organizations for information about environmental policies.

Students will prepare a questionnaire to survey members of the community about their ability and willingness to change their way of life to benefit the environment. What habits would people willingly change? Would they give up some comforts and recreation to improve the environment? The class will tally and evaluate the results of the survey.

Next students will work with a multimedia software program. Earthquest Explores Ecology is a HyperCard stack overflowing with sound, animation, games, charts, graphs, and simulations. The program provides information about all facets of life on Earth as well as an introduction to HyperCard, and is available for both Macintosh and DOS computers.

After using Earthquest students will write a HyperfCard stack using the information from their research. This HyperCard stack may be added to the library collection and used by other classes.

Resources

BOOKS

Conservation Directory. Washington, D.C.: National Wildlife Federation, 1991.

Elkington, John, Julia Hailes, Douglas Hill, and Joel Makower. *Going Green: A Kid's Handbook to Saving the Planet*. New York: Viking, 1990.

Farmer, Lesley, and Jean Hewitt. *I Speak HyperCard*. Englewood, Colo.: Libraries Unlimited, 1992.

50 Simple Things You Can Do to Save the Earth. Berkeley, Calif.: The Earthworks Press, 1989.

Gold, Rebecca. *HyperCard 2 QuickStart*. Carmel, Ind.: Que, 1992.

Schwartz, Linda. *Earth Book for Kids*. Santa Barbara, Calif.: Learning Works, 1990.

VIDEOS

Fern Gully—The Last Rainforest. 20th Century Fox, 1992.

Help Save the Planet Earth. MCA Universal Home Video, 1990. With Ted Danson, Whoopi Goldberg, and others. Extensive information about agencies and other resources.

TELECOMMUNICATIONS NETWORKS

America Online, 8619 Westwood Center Dr., Vienna, VA 22182; 800-827-6364. Environment Forum.

CompuServe, 5000 Arlington Centre Blvd., P.O. Box 20212, Columbus, OH 43220; 800-848-8990. Earth Forum.

Econet, 18 de Boom St., San Francisco, CA 94107; 415-442-0220.

These forums provide information about all aspects of the environment, including wildlife, recycling, animal rights, and lands and forests.

AGENCIES

Clean Water Action, 317 Pennsylvania Ave., SE, Washington, DC 20003.

Environmental Action Foundation, 1525 New Hampshire Ave., NW, Washington, D.C. 20036; 202-745-4870.

Environmental Defense Fund, 257 Park Ave. South, New York, NY 10010; 212-505-2100.

Environmental Policy Institute, 218 D St., SE, Washington, D.C. 20003; 202-544-2600.

Global Tomorrow Coalition, 1325 G St., NW, Suite 915, Washington, D.C. 20005; 202-628-4016.

Greenpeace USA, 1436 U St., NW, Washington, DC 20009; 202-462-1177.

National Audubon Society, 700 Broadway, New York, NY 10003; 212-979-3000.

National Recycling Coalition, 1105 30th St., NW, Washington, DC 20007; 202-625-6406.

National Wildlife Federation, 1400 16th St., NW, Washington, DC 20036-2266; 703-790-4343.

Natural Resources Defense Council, 40 W. 20th St., New York, NY 10011; 212-727-4400.

Office of Community and Intergovernmental Relations (A-108 EA). U.S. Environmental Protection Agency, 401 M St., SW, Washington, D.C. 20460; 202-382-4454.

Plastics Recycling Foundation, 1275 K St., NW, Suite 400, Washington, DC 20005; 202-371-5200.

The RCRA Information Center, U.S. Environmental Protection Agency, 401 M St., SW, Washington, DC 20460. The Recycle Today educational program consists of publications for classroom use. Available material includes a curriculum book with classroom activities and projects, a handbook describing school recycling programs, a poster, and a comic book. Free.

Sierra Club, 730 Polk St., San Francisco, CA 94109; 415-776-2211.

Office of Environmental Awareness, S. Dillon Ripley Center, Room 3123, MRC 705.

Smithsonian Institution, Washington, DC 20560. For information about threatened and endangered animals.

Notes

1. "Natural Resources: Can They Be Saved?" *Popular Science* 241 (July 1992): 8-10.

Teaching Plan I: Planning the Research (Worksheets 6.1, 6.2, and 6.3)

Materials: Library catalog, encyclopedias, *Readers' Guide to Periodical Literature*, the *New Grolier Multimedia Encyclopedia*, computer with CD-ROM player.

Teaching Strategy: This project may be used as part of an integrated curriculum for science, social studies, and communication arts. The discussion of human behavior and its effect on the environment will begin in the classroom before the first library visit. Students will read encyclopedia articles and use the library catalog to find background information.

Worksheet 6.1 is a guide for developing a search strategy. Students will work in small groups, using *Readers' Guide* and other resources to develop a list of subject headings and a work plan. Students will complete practice exercises (worksheet 6.2) before they begin to research their topics. Students will use worksheet 6.3 while working with the electronic encyclopedia. A list of agencies to write to ask for additional information is provided.

Information on using the *Readers' Guide to Periodical Literature* appears on worksheet 4.1 (pages 47-48).

Teaching Plan II: The Community and the Environment (Worksheets 6.4 and 6.5)

Materials: Survey questionnaire developed for this activity, evaluation and tally forms.

Teaching Strategy: Students will survey members of the community to determine how their behavior affects the environment, what changes in their behavior can improve the environment, and whether people are willing to make those changes.

Sample questions are listed on worksheet 6.4. Students will be encouraged to suggest additional survey questions during class discussions. After the survey is conducted, students will use worksheet 6.5 to analyze and evaluate the data. A group of students from a math class will tally the survey results and present them to the class.

Teaching Plan III: HyperCard (Worksheets 6.6 and 6.7)

Materials: Earthquest Explores Ecology or Earthtreks, HyperCard, computer, printer, students' plans for authoring an ecology stack.

Teaching Strategy: Students will use Earthquest Explores Ecology or Earthtreks to get additional information for their research projects. The program manual defines the buttons used, and these should be reviewed with the class prior to use. Students will work in groups, following the instructions given on worksheet 6.6. They will use the notebook option to take and save notes. Worksheet 6.7 defines HyperCard terms and provides basic information on how to build a HyperCard stack.

Each group of students will contribute cards for the stack after submitting a plan that indicates what information the group will include and how the buttons will be used to link the cards. Before groups begin work the class should meet to exchange information about the cards each group plans to create for the stack and how the cards will be connected to each other. Before attempting to author cards, students should use the introductory and help stacks that come with the software. Students will use problem-solving skills as they browse through the introductory stacks, creating new cards as they go.

Worksheet 6.1: Planning a Research Project

How do we balance the needs of people with those of the natural world? You have learned during classroom discussion that the way in which people relate to nature is part of their way of life and is not always easy to change. A person's livelihood or food supply may be at stake when we try to save the rain forests, curb the lumber industry, or prevent the killing of endangered animals. This research project deals with the effect of human behavior on the environment. Think about which aspect of the problem you are most interested in researching. You may need to do additional reading before you decide on your research topic. If you need more information, read an encyclopedia article and use the library catalog to find books to read before you begin your research. Think about the following questions to get started:

- Is it possible for people to survive economically while conserving endangered species?
- Is it right to ask poor farmers in the Amazon rain forest to stop contributing to the destruction of the land if this is how they earn their livelihood?
- Is it possible for animals threatened with extinction to recover?
- Is the endangerment or extinction of a species simply part of evolution?
- Are all ecological changes caused by humans bad?
- Is it possible for people to change habits that are part of their culture in order to help the environment?

DEVELOPING THE RESEARCH QUESTION

You have been discussing the issue of the environment and culture in class and are now ready to begin your research. Ask yourself, What do I want to find out about this subject? Does something particularly interest me, for example, an endangered species or a part of the world that I want to learn more about? To develop a research question, complete the following steps.

1. List the subjects that you want to research.
2. Develop two or three questions about these subjects. Make the questions broad enough to use as research topics.
3. List the key words found in your research question.
4. Using dictionaries and a thesaurus, find synonyms for the key words in your questions.
5. Find the key words and synonyms in *Readers' Guide to Periodical Literature* to find related topics and current issues about the subject.
6. Write your research questions using the key words and synonyms.

Worksheet 6.2: Using the New Grolier Multimedia Encyclopedia

The *New Grolier Multimedia Encyclopedia* on CD-ROM is the complete *Academic American Encyclopedia* on one CD-ROM disc. There are three ways to search for information using the electronic encyclopedia's search menu: the TITLE INDEX, the WORD INDEX, and the general WORD SEARCH. The search menu also includes a picture index and a map index.

TITLE INDEX

The TITLE INDEX is an alphabetical list of every article in the electronic encyclopedia. Click on TITLE INDEX.

For practice, at the SEARCH MENU, type ATOMIC BOMB to see the article on this subject. Notice the boxes and icons that appear above the article. Click on them to see the kinds of information they contain or what they allow you to do. Close to exit the article. Go back to the SEARCH MENU.

WORD INDEX

This is an alphabetical list of every word in the electronic encyclopedia. To use the WORD INDEX type the word you want to find. You are shown in how many articles the word appears and the number of times it appears in the encyclopedia.

For practice, at the SEARCH MENU, click on the WORD INDEX. Type ATOMIC.

In how many articles does this word appear? How many times does it appear in the electronic encyclopedia?

Double-click on ATOMIC to see a title list of articles in which the word appears. Go back to the WORD INDEX. Erase ATOMIC.

Type BOMB. In how many articles does this word appear? How many times does it appear in the electronic encyclopedia?

Double-click on BOMB to see a title list of articles in which the word appears. Go back to the SEARCH MENU.

WORD SEARCH

This option allows you to search for any word with or without other words. The combinations of words will broaden or narrow your search. If your research question is too broad, you will get more information than you need. If the question is too narrow, you will not have enough information for your research.

To practice at the SEARCH MENU click on WORD SEARCH. On the first line type ATOMIC. How many articles appear in the title list? Close the title list. Erase ATOMIC.

Type BOMB on the first line. How many articles appear in this title list? Close the title list. Erase BOMB.

Now type ATOMIC BOMB on the first line. How many articles appear in this title list? Why does ATOMIC BOMB produce a smaller number of articles, or a narrower search, than ATOMIC or BOMB alone? Close the title list.

Start again. Type ATOMIC on the first line and BOMB on the second. What happens to the number of articles? Why?

Start again. On the first line type ATOMIC BOMB and on the second line type WORLD WAR II. How many articles do you find? Why?

(Worksheet 6.2– continued)

Start again. On the first line type ATOMIC BOMB. Change the plus sign on the second line to a minus sign and type WORLD WAR II. What happened to your title list?

Start again. Type ATOMIC BOMB on the first line and WAR on the second. What happened?

Experiment with the WORD SEARCH option to see how topics become broader and narrower depending on where the words are typed and which modifiers (plus and minus signs) are used.

PICTURE INDEX

The PICTURE INDEX is an alphabetical listing of pictures in the electronic encyclopedia. For practice, at the SEARCH MENU click on PICTURE INDEX. Scroll and find MAMMALS. Click on BABOON. Notice the audio icon to the left of the illustration. Click it to hear the baboon.

Go back to the PICTURE INDEX and click on the name of an animal of your choosing. Notice that audio is not available for all pictures.

What icon shows that there is sound available?

MAP INDEX

The MAP INDEX is an alphabetical list of maps in the electronic encyclopedia. For practice, at the SEARCH MENU click on MAP INDEX. Scroll. Click on IRELAND to find that map. Repeat for INDIA and FRANCE.

FEATURES OF THE ENCYCLOPEDIA

To get the most out of the electronic encyclopedia, you must be able to use four main features: the title list, icons, linking cross references, and the notepad.

Title List

The title list is a list of titles of articles that results from a search using the word index or word search. The articles in the title list contain the word or combination of words used in your search. You can double click on each title to see the full article.

Icons

The following icons appear above some of the articles:

Outline icon. Appears when the article is a long one. Clicking on this icon lets you find the information you are looking for more easily. This gives a detailed outline of the subject allowing you to select more specific information.

Factbox. A list of standard facts about the person, object, or country that is the subject of the article.

Table. Statistical information. Available in some articles by clicking the icon.

(Worksheet 6.2—continued)

Bibliography. Books to read for more information. The bibliography appears at the end of the article, but clicking on the icon will let you jump to it.

Audio. Indicates sound is available. Click on it to hear the sound.

Camera. A picture can be accessed by clicking this icon.

Linking Cross References

Sometimes when you are reading an article you will find something of particular interest to you. You may go to other articles on the same subject by linking cross references, which appear in all capital letters.

For practice, at the SEARCH MENU click on WORD SEARCH. Type ENDANGERED SPECIES.

Find the paragraph on whales. Highlight the word WHALES. From the SEARCH MENU choose HYPERLINK to SELECTION. The article on whaling now appears.

Notepad

When you open a NOTEPAD on the file menu, you can copy whole or parts of articles or write your own research notes. These notes can be printed directly or saved and printed later.

For practice, at the SEARCH MENU click on WORD SEARCH. Type ATOMIC BOMB on the first line. Open the first article and highlight any part of it.

Select COPY from the EDIT MENU. Open NEW NOTEPAD from the FILE MENU. Two windows are now on your screen: the highlighted article and the untitled notepad.

Select PASTE from the EDIT MENU. The highlighted part of the article now appears in the notepad. To save your notepad, select SAVE from the FILE MENU and give your file a name. You may save to the hard drive or a floppy disk.

You can write notes to your notepad. For practice write a memo to yourself and save it.

To add more information to the same file at a later time, use OPEN NOTEPAD from the FILE MENU.

These instructions for the electronic encyclopedia are very basic. As you become accustomed to using the electronic encyclopedia, you will learn to use additional search techniques and options.

Worksheet 6.3: Electronic Encyclopedia Activity Sheet

Complete the following steps to research your topic on an electronic encyclopedia.

1. What are your research questions?

2. List the key words in the research questions.
3. Use WORD SEARCH to find articles that include these key words.
4. Search the title list to find the articles that will give you the information you need. Double click to open each article. Read the articles. Highlight the information you need.
5. Create a notepad. Copy portions of articles or take notes. Be sure to save the file. To open the notepad file later, use OPEN NOTEPAD from the FILE MENU.
6. Check bibliographies for more information sources. At the end of each article is a bibliography. Be sure to read this list to see if you can find additional material for your topic.
7. Use cross references (linking) to obtain more information.
8. As you do your research, you will probably find information that interests you but doesn't answer the original research questions. Don't limit yourself to only those questions. Be flexible, and if you need to broaden your topic, do so.

Worksheet 6.4: Community Survey: The Environment

Your class has been doing research on the effect of human behavior on the environment. We know that no place on Earth exists in isolation and that ignoring conservation in any one part of the world affects the rest of the world. We may find it difficult to understand how people in a remote part of the world can misuse nature, but are people in your own community willing to change their habits to benefit the environment? This survey will be conducted in your neighborhood or your school to find out whether the people you know are willing to change their habits. Discuss the survey questions in class and change them or add to them to suit your community. Make copies of the survey form and pass them out to as many people as possible. The surveys should be returned completed to the students who distributed them.

Community Survey on the Environment

This survey is being conducted to determine what is being done in your community to improve the environment and to find out if people are willing to change their habits to help the environment. Please answer all questions carefully and honestly. Thank you.

Age group (circle one): Child Teen Adult

Sex (circle one): Male Female

Transportation

1. Do you use mass transit? How frequently?
2. If you answered no, why not?
3. If you do not use mass transit what, if any, changes in the mass transit system would induce you to give up your automobile and use public transportation?
4. Do you ever carpool? How frequently?
5. Would you be willing to carpool to reduce pollution?
6. Do you ever use a bicycle or walk rather than use your car to reduce pollution? How often?

Comments:

(Worksheet 6.4—continued)

Shopping

1. Do you make a conscious effort to use only biodegradable, recycled, or environmentally sound products?
   a. If yes, which products?
   b. If no, why not?
2. Do you avoid buying products that use unnecessary plastic wrapping?
3. Do you reuse shopping bags and containers?
4. Can you share with us some ways you shop that are environmentally sound?
5. If you knew that some of your shopping habits were environmentally unsound would you change your way of shopping?

Comments:

Recycling

1. Do you recycle products at home?
2. Which of the following do you regularly recycle? (Circle one.)

   Clothing   Paper containers and bags   Aluminum foil   Plastic containers and bags
3. Is there a voluntary recycling program in your community?
4. Do you take part in it?
5. Do you think it should be a mandatory program?
6. Do you think most people would be upset about having to comply with the rules of a mandatory recycling program? Why or why not?

Comments:

Nature

1. Do you follow instructions carefully and minimize the use of herbicides and pesticides?
2. Do you try to reduce runoff of pesticides with good grass cover and shrubs?
3. Do you know how to make a compost pile?

(Worksheet 6.4—continued)

4. Would you be willing to save your food wastes to use in a compost pile?
5. Do you put lawn clippings and garden weeds into compost piles to improve the soil in your garden?
6. How important do you think it is to help the environment in these ways?

   Very important   Somewhat important   Not at all important

7. If you became aware of the importance of doing these things, would you begin to change your habits, even if it took extra time and effort? If no, why not?

Comments:

Energy

1. Do you use energy-efficient appliances? Which ones?
2. Do you ever use compact fluorescent bulbs rather than standard light bulbs to conserve energy?
3. Do you make a conscious effort to turn out lights when you leave a room or try to use the air conditioner less frequently?
4. Have you set back your thermostat to conserve energy?
5. Are you willing to change any unsound habits to help conserve energy? Which ones?
6. Would you be willing to pay more for electric power if it produced cleaner air?

Comments:

Air Pollution

1. Have you had your home tested for radon?
2. Are you aware of the following indoor pollutants? (Circle them.)

Formaldehyde in new furniture	Pesticides	Aerosols
Dry cleaning solvents	Tobacco smoke	Scented products
Gas appliances	Heaters	Cleaning products
Synthetic fibers in carpets and drapes	Vacuum cleaners	

(Worksheet 6.4—continued)

3. Have you curbed your use of any these pollutants? Which ones?

4. Are you willing to change your use of these pollutants? Which ones?

5. Are you aware that some house plants, such as the spider plant and philodendron, will remove some pollutants from indoor air?

Comments:

Waste Disposal

Toxic waste may pollute the water supply if dumped down a drain. Batteries contain hazardous material that can leak at landfills and get into the water supply.

1. Do you use rechargeable batteries wherever possible?
2. If not, do you throw your batteries away at a waste site?
3. Does your community have a drop-off site for hazardous waste?
4. If not, would you help to organize a hazardous waste disposal day in your neighborhood?

Comments:

Worksheet 6.5: Analyzing the Survey Results

Number of people surveyed:

Number in each age group: Child Teen Adult

Number of each sex: Male Female

Transportation

1. How many adults use mass transit regularly? Occasionally?
2. How many adults carpool, use bicycles, or walk regularly? Occasionally?
3. How many are willing to change? How many are most willing to change to mass transit? Carpool? Bike? Walking?

Comments:

Shopping

1. Which biodegradable products do people regularly use?

2. Are people willing to change their shopping habits? Explain.

Recycling

1. If there is a recycling center in your community, how many people use it?
2. How many people recycle products at home?
3. Which products do they recycle?
4. How many people interviewed are willing to begin recycling now?
5. How many people believe there should be a mandatory recycling program in the community if none exists now?

Nature

1. How many people feel it is very important, important, and not important to help in the ways mentioned in the survey?
2. How many are willing to change their habits?

Comments:

(Worksheet 6.5—continued)

Energy

1. Which energy-efficient appliances are people using?

2. In what other ways are they helping to conserve energy?

Comments:

Air Pollution

1. How many adults have had their homes tested for radon?
2. Which indoor pollutants do people use most often?

3. Which are they willing to do without or use less frequently?

Comments:

Waste Disposal

1. If a hazardous waste disposal site is available in the community, how many people use it?
2. How many are willing to start a community hazardous waste disposal day?
3. Are people aware of hazardous wastes in their homes?

Comments:

Evaluation

1. Which of the following habits are the people in your community most willing to change to help the environment? (Circle them.)

Transportation	Shopping	Recycling
Use of Nature	Energy	Air Pollution

(Worksheet 6.5—continued)

2. Which of the following habits are the most difficult to change? (Circle them.)

Transportation	Shopping	Recycling
Use of Nature	Energy	Air Pollution

3. Why do you think this is true?

4. Is there a difference between children, teens, and adults in their willingness to change?

   a. What is that difference?

   b. If there is a difference, why do you think this is so?

5. Do you think the people in your community are aware of the potential danger of some of their habits?

6. What can be done to make them more aware of the problem of environmental pollution?

Worksheet 6.6: Earthquest Explores Ecology

Earthquest Explores Ecology is a HyperCard stack that explores ecology using text, animation, graphics, and sound. It lets you save your research in a notebook using text and graphics. Earthquest is fun to use on your own, but it takes some experimenting, and you may get lost at first. Keep exploring, and you will find lots of information for your research. Don't forget to click on the icons at the bottom of the screens as you go along.

Answering the questions below will help you find your way around Earthquest. But don't stop there. Keep exploring. Use the notebook on the Ecooptions Menu to save your notes. Good luck and have fun!

Three maps lead to everything in the ecosystem. They are: Ecoexplorer, Ecosystems, and Rain Forest Explorer. Important features of the program are the Workshop, Carrot Cruiser, and Renegade Tour.

USING THE ECOEXPLORER MAP

1. Click on GLOSSARY to find definitions for the following terms.

   Species—

   Toxins—

   Social groups—

2. Find other definitions you need for your research.
3. Use the bibliography to find three books that may be helpful in your research. List the authors and titles.
4. Find the name and address of an organization from whom you may request information for your research. Write the name and address here.

Return to the ECOEXPLORER MAP. Click on PLANTS/ANIMALS—ADAPTATION. Click the first icon on the bottom left.

1. Define *adaptation.*
2. Name two kinds of *adaptation*.
3. Click on the picture of the bear. What is the difference between *carnivores, omnivores, herbivores*?

Return to the ECOEXPLORER MAP. Click on WONDERS OF NATURE. Read about the various relationships in an ecosystem. Click on the ones you want to read about.

(Worksheet 6.6—continued)

USING THE ECOSYSTEMS MAP

Find the BIOME MAP, click on it, and answer the questions:

1. What is a *biome*? How many land and water biomes are used in this program? Name them.

2. Select two biomes that are most useful for your research and describe them.

3. Find the TROPICAL RAIN FOREST biome. Click on it. Click on the help icon and read about ways to help save the rain forest. What is Rain Forest Crunch?

4. Click on PLACES TO EXPLORE. What is a World Heritage Site?

5. Click on ECOEXPERIMENTS. Print an experiment that will help you with your research.

USING THE RAIN FOREST EXPLORER MAP

1. Click on ENDANGERED RAINFOREST. List three important features of the rain forest.

   a.

   b.

   c.

USING WORKSHOP

Go to WORKSHOP and follow the directions. You will be able to make animated screens.

USING CARROT CRUISER AND RENEGADE TOUR

Don't forget the CARROT CRUISER and the RENEGADE TOUR to find challenging ecology games.

Worksheet 6.7: Working with HyperCard

Earthquest Explores Ecology introduced you to HyperCard stacks. You browsed through the cards, used the buttons, saved notes, and used the workshop. Now it's time to write your own stack using the information you gathered from your research. Each group will contribute cards to the stack.

There are many versions of HyperCard. The newer versions have added features, but the basics remain the same. Whatever version of HyperCard you are using, start at the beginning and go through all the introductory information.

PREFERENCE LEVELS

HyperCard is divided into five user levels, starting from the simplest and working up. Before you start to write your own stack, you must go through the introductory stack and help stack that came with the version of HyperCard that you are using. It is very important to start at the easiest level and work up to the hardest without skipping anything. The five levels are:

Browsing. This is what you did when you used Earthquest. You used the buttons to link information and the arrows to go back and forth within the program, but you did not change the stack in any way.

Typing. At this level you can enter, add, delete, and edit text information onto a card. Practice doing this before you go on to the next level.

Painting. This level allows you to create and edit graphics. You can use the paint tools for this, or you can copy pictures from another program. This allows you to illustrate your research with graphics that you select or draw. Additional menus are added at this level: PAINT, OPTIONS, and PATTERNS. Use the tools to experiment. Don't be afraid to make mistakes.

Authoring. This is where the real fun begins. This level allows to change things around, making the stack look exactly as you want it to look and designing your own buttons and fields by modifying parts of the stacks that came with HyperCard. At this level you can use your research and graphics to illustrate your stack.

Scripting or HyperTalk. This is the most advanced level. You can create your own stack, writing scripts in a language called HyperTalk. You must go through all the other levels before you try this one.

GLOSSARY: HYPERCARD

Background. A background may be shared by many cards. A background is made up of the background picture, fields, and buttons. The background for a stack containing names and addresses would be 1) name (this is entered on all cards in the stack, but each card would have a different name and address); and 2) address.

Browse tool. An icon that is used for direction and writing. The browse tool changes appearance depending on where it is on the screen. Sometimes it looks like a little hand.

Button. A button connects two or more cards. Use the button tool from the TOOLS MENU to create a button.

Card. A card is the basic unit of information. It may contain text, sound, graphics, or animation. Think of it as a 5-by-7-inch index card.

(Worksheet 6.7—continued)

Field. The field is an area that contains text and changes from card to card. Use the field tool from the TOOLS MENU.

Home card. A picture map of a stack.

Stack. A HyperCard program is called a stack. A stack is made up of a collection of cards, which usually are about one subject. You are going to write a stack about the environment using your research. Every group in the class will contribute cards to this stack.

But don't stop here. These are only the very basics and they don't nearly do justice to the many fascinating things that you can create using this software. But the only way to become an expert at HyperCard is by using it, experimenting, and creating. You will discover many things that have not been discussed here by thoroughly using the stacks and manual that came with your HyperCard software.

PLANNING YOUR STACK

After using the introductory stack and help stack and working through the browsing, typing, and painting user levels, you will be ready to use the authoring level. Planning is important. Discuss the following with your group.

1. What information will be included on each card?
2. What will the background card be?
3. Will graphics be used? Will you use the paint tools to create your own pictures or import pictures from another stack or paint program?
4. How many cards will you need?
5. How many buttons will you use?

Information in Modern Society: Reading, Viewing, and Searching

This is the age of the information explosion, so much to know, so much to find out about that it's bound to be overwhelming. But the ways in which people receive information has always been in a state of evolution. Prehistoric people drew pictures on cave walls; smoke signals, drum beats, and town criers have delivered news. The image of Paul Revere is etched on all our minds. The printing press, telegraph, and railroad sped the delivery of information and increased the amount of information people needed. Today, the information available to us, and the information we need, comes from around the world, and the faster we get it the better.

Not so long ago newspapers were the primary medium for news. However, newspapers have been in decline for some time, and for many of us they are no longer a major source of news. When we want to hear the latest news, we turn to television or radio. Television not only tells but shows us if our team won the game, prepares us for tomorrow's weather, and gossips about our favorite celebrities. It informs and entertains us.

Commercial information networks, such as CompuServe,[1] are providing additional ways to obtain information. These networks offers a plethora of online features, ranging from financial reports to weather reports, news services, online encyclopedias and databases, games, travel, shopping, and sports—all at a price. Knowledge is power, and finding information in a modern technological society may cost several dollars per hour.

The projects in this chapter lead students through the hierarchy of information resources, from newspapers to television to the electronic wonderland of online services like CompuServe. Table 7.1 gives a timetable for each project.

The social studies or language arts teacher, working with the librarian, will discuss with students the notion of information as a commodity and the many ways we obtain it. Students will brainstorm about where information comes from; they will understand that information equals power and that access to information does not always come cheap. Students will begin by exploring an inexpensive source of information, the daily newspaper. They will discuss the importance and various components of newspapers and will understand how facts can become distorted and changed into opinions. Students will next turn to television. Television news has become the country's most important source of information, shaping the way we view the world. Students will watch a newscast and compare it to newspapers as to clarity and depth of coverage.

Next, students will use CompuServe. CompuServe charges a monthly fee for access to many basic services, plus an additional charge for access to most databases and forums. However, $150 per school year will provide enough online time for learning and using the basics. It is very important to control costs. Without careful preparation, scheduling, and supervision, students can get lost in an expensive electronic maze that can prove addictive. Teachers and librarians should be familiar with menus and commands before students are allowed near the computer. To acquaint students with the system, give them a list of questions and instructions for finding the answers. It is instructive to have students print a copy of the charges for each online session. This not only keeps track of costs but helps students understand the expense involved.

Next, students will evaluate and analyze the information network, comparing it to newspapers and television as a source of information.

Notes

1. CompuServe, 5000 Arlington Centre Blvd., P.O. Box 20212, Columbus, OH 43220. 1-800-848-8199.

Teaching Plan I: Newspapers and Television (Worksheets 7.1, 7.2, and 7.3)

Materials: Books about communications and information; a class set of newspapers or, if possible,

Table 7.1
Timetable for Information in Modern Society

Project	Number of Library Periods	Number of Class Periods
Newspapers and Television		
Worksheet 7.1: Newspapers		4
Worksheet 7.2: Television Newscasts	4	
Worksheet 7.3: Comparing Television and Newspapers		2
Information Networks		
Worksheet 7.4: Information Networks	1	
Worksheet 7.5: Using CompuServe	6 (per group)	
Worksheet 7.6: Comparing and Evaluating Newspapers, Television, and Information Networks		2
Total	5 +6 (per group)	8

one class set of each of two newspapers; and a videotaped television newscast.

Teaching Strategy: The class will discuss how people have obtained information in the past, how the delivery of information has evolved, and how its delivery is being changed by new technology. Students will use the school library to find books describing early communications systems and about the history of newspapers. They will research the processes involved in producing a newspaper and television newscast. If possible, the class will visit a local television station or newspaper, or the editor of the local newspaper or producer of a local news program will speak to the class.

Using worksheet 7.1, students will read and identify the various parts of a newspaper. It may be necessary for the teacher to read aloud from the newspaper. The class will be assigned to view a television newscast, and that newscast will be videotaped for repeated viewing in class. (The newspaper and the newscast must cover the same news stories to make the comparison meaningful.) Using worksheet 7.2, students will identify the parts of a television newscast and analyze the newscast. Using worksheet 7.3, students will examine and contrast the content of the newspaper and the assigned newscast. Each worksheet will be accompanied by class discussion and evaluation of the assigned stories.

Teaching Plan II: Information Networks (Worksheets 7.4, 7.5, and 7.6)

Materials: Computer; modem; printer; subscription to a commercial information network, such as CompuServe; directions for accessing the network using the available equipment and software.

Teaching Strategy: Students will be familiar with the use of the computer, modem, and software before going online. The class will discuss the ways in which technology has changed the delivery of information and how that change has affected our lives. Groups of four or five students will use the computer, with the librarian or teacher available to offer assistance. Worksheet 7.4 describes information networks. Worksheet 7.5 provides questions to familiarize students with some of the basic services available on CompuServe. If funds are available students will explore Student Forum, Information USA, Iquest, and similar services. Although charges are not immediately available for the present session, each group will print a copy of charges each time it completes an online session to show students how much the service costs. Using worksheet 7.6 students will evaluate each of the information sources used. A class discussion will follow.

Worksheet 7.1: Newspapers

Since the beginning of time people have communicated information. Prehistoric people drew pictures on cave walls, and ancient peoples communicated through writing. Scribes copied books by hand. Information was spread by word of mouth and by town criers. People who traveled from place to place carried news with them. The printing press made it possible to bring more and more information to greater numbers of people through newspapers and magazines. The telegraph and the railroad helped speed the relaying of information. Today radio and television are the most popular ways of quickly finding out what we want to know.

Newspapers remain one of the easiest-to-use tools to find the information we need. We read newspapers to find out what is going on in the world, the country, and our community, but we also read newspapers for other kinds of information. The television page tells us what shows are on and when, movie reviews clue us into recent openings that we might or might not think are worth seeing. Advertisements let us know what is on sale; classified ads help us find a job or a new car; and sports, fashion, and the daily horoscope make newspapers fun to read. Finally, we can carry a newspaper with us wherever we go and read it whenever we want.

This worksheet will help you learn about the various sections of a newspaper.

QUESTIONS: INFORMATION

1. Find a definition of *information* in a dictionary. Copy it here.

2. How does information differ from knowledge?

3. We all have ways of finding out about things that are important to us. Name some of the ways that you find information.

PARTS OF A NEWS ARTICLE

All news articles contain similar information arranged in a similar format.

Lead

All news articles have a lead, one or two paragraphs that summarize the story by answering some or all of the questions: Who? What? When? Where? Why? and How? Read a lead in your newspaper and answer as many of the following questions as you can.

1. Who are the people mentioned in the article?

2. What event is described?

3. When did the event take place?

(Worksheet 7.1—continued)

4. Where did it take place?
5. Why did it happen?
6. How did it happen?

Body

1. After the lead, the body of the article describes all the important facts in detail. Continue reading the story and list all the important facts.

Last Paragraph

The least important parts of a news article are in the last paragraph.

1. Briefly list some of the less important facts in the article.
2. Could you have understood the story without this paragraph?

PARTS OF A NEWSPAPER

All newspapers have certain characteristics in common. However, some newspapers concentrate on local news while others are more concerned with international and national events. Many newspapers subscribe to news services that have reporters around the world; the reporters provide the news services with news from many cities and countries around the world, and subscribing newspapers purchase the articles from the news service. Read your newspaper to find the following parts.

Front Page

This is the most important page of any newspaper. The following features are usually found on the front page.

Name of the Newspaper and Date

What is the name of the newspaper you are reading for this project? What is the date?

Top Story

The most important article of the day is called the top story and is given the biggest headline.

1. What is the biggest headline on the front page?
2. How do you think an editor decides which is the most important story of the day?

(Worksheet 7.1—continued)

Index

The index tells you where to find the information you are looking for; it is usually found on the front page.

1. How is the index arranged?
2. Use the index to find your favorite section of the newspaper. What page(s) is this section on?

Editorial Page

Use the index to help you find the editorial page. An editorial expresses the opinions of the editors of the newspaper. An opinion tells how a person feels about something, but a fact can be proven. However, a fact can be turned into an opinion with the addition of just a few words. Opinions are supposed to appear only on the editorial page, not in news articles. Turn to the editorial page and read an editorial.

1. What issue is discussed?
2. What opinion is expressed?
3. Do you agree or disagree with this opinion? Explain.

Letters to the Editor

Letters to the Editor appear on the editorial pages. In letters readers express their opinions about issues. Sometimes the letters are replies to an editorial or to letters that appeared earlier. Read a letter in this section and summarize the contents.

Summary:

Political Columns

Political columns are found on the editorial pages. These columns are written by experts who give their opinions about political events. Read a political column in your newspaper and answer the following.

1. Who wrote the column?
2. What is the column about?
3. What opinion is expressed?
4. Do you agree or disagree with the opinion? Why?

(Worksheet 7.1—continued)

Political Cartoons

Political cartoons appear on the editorial pages because they express an opinion. Not all newspapers include cartoons. If there is a cartoon in your newspaper, answer the following questions.

1. Who drew it?
2. What is the cartoon about?
3. How is the cartoonist's opinion expressed?

News Articles

Newspapers are supposed to express opinions or editorialize only on the editorial pages. However, very often opinions appear in news articles as well. Read a news article and find words that express an opinion.

1. Explain how the words make the sentences in which they are used opinion and not fact.

2. Read the following sentences. Explain why each is a fact or opinion.

   a. Gun control will reduce crime.

   b. All television advertising is deceptive.

   c. An uncontrollable mob was demonstrating at the mall today.

   d. Cigarette smoking must be banned in all public places to ensure public health.

   e. You must be 35 years old to become a United States president.

   f. People are in a panic as they await the destructive hurricane.

   g. There is evidence that secondhand smoke causes lung cancer.

   h. Homeless people are too lazy to work.

   i. The Russians were the first in outer space.

(Worksheet 7.1—continued)

3. Rewrite the above sentences changing the facts into opinions and the opinions into facts.

Photographs

Photographs draw readers' attention; almost all newspapers use them.

1. Find a photograph in the newspaper and explain how it helps you understand the story.

Other Sections

Newspapers also print sports, business, entertainment, fashion, and science articles. These articles are collected in sections, or groups of pages, devoted to the topic. Each section features a top story. Select one of these sections. Use the index to find the section you selected. Read the top story.

1. Who wrote the article?
2. What is the article about?
3. Where did the events described take place?
4. When did the events take place?
5. If this is a subject that you know about, was the report accurate? Explain.

Other Features

1. Which of these features appear in your newspaper?

   Puzzles Horoscopes Weather

   Comics TV schedules Advice columns

   Movie and theater reviews Classified advertisements

2. Which of these do you regularly read?
3. Do you think this newspaper is writing for a particular audience? Explain.
4. Does this newspaper feature more international, national, or local news on the front page?
5. Do you think it is important for newspapers to feature more local, national, or international news? Why?
6. Is this newspaper exciting to read? Why?

Worksheet 7.2: Television Newscasts

Today people learn the latest news very differently than they did just a short time ago. Until regular network television broadcasts began in 1940, most people learned about current events from newspapers and radio. Today television newscasts bring us the latest news as well as sports, interviews, weather, and business reports. For this assignment you will watch a television newscast, paying close attention to it.

QUESTIONS

Parts of a Television Newscast

Watch the videotaped newscast and time the various segments.

1. How long is the newscast?
2. How much time was spent on the top story?
3. If interviews were part of the story, how many and how long were they? How much time was spent on national news? World news? Local news?
4. How much time was spent on the following?

Weather	Sports	Entertainment
Science or Health	Other features	

5. Do you think enough time was given to the top story?
6. Do you think too much time was given to features such as weather and sports? Explain and discuss.

Commercials

Commercials are important because they pay for the newscast. Advertisers pay for the program in the hope that you will go out and buy their products.

1. How much time was given to the commercials?
2. How many commercials were there?
3. Do you think that the show had too many commercials? Explain.
4. Do you usually pay attention to commercials?
5. Name the products that were advertised on this newscast.
6. Was there a reason for these products to be advertised at this time? Explain.

(Worksheet 7.2—continued)

7. Were the commercials informative? Explain.

8. Did the commercials interfere with the news program? In what way?

9. Do you think the claims made in the commercials are accurate? Explain.

Watching a Television Newscast

The people on a newscast who read the news and introduce the stories are called anchors.

1. Describe the anchor people.
2. Do the anchor people or reporters give opinions about the news?
3. Do they tell you that it is an opinion? If not, how do you know that they are expressing their opinions?

Summarize the following stories. Describe the visual presentation. Tell what the story was about, who were the people involved, and where and when it took place. How did it happen and why? Include any descriptive words that were used.

1. Top story

Summary of story:

a. Did the reporter's questions encourage the person interviewed to tell the story? Was there enough time for the interview?

b. How did the interview enhance the story?

c. How did the film help you understand the story? How did the film influence your opinion about the news story?

d. Was music used? How did the music influence your feelings?

2. World news

Summary of story:

a. Did the reporter's questions encourage the person interviewed to tell the story? Was there enough time for the interview?

(Worksheet 7.2—continued)

b. How did the interview enhance the story?

c. How did the film help you understand the story?

d. How did the film influence your opinion about the news story?

e. Was music used? How did the music influence your feelings?

3. National news

Summary of story:

a. Did the reporter's questions encourage the person interviewed to tell the story? Was there enough time for the interview?

b. How did the interview enhance the story?

c. How did the film help you understand the story?

d. How did the film influence your opinion about the news story?

e. Was music used? How did the music influence your feelings?

4. Local news

Summary of story:

a. Did the reporter's questions encourage the person interviewed to tell the story? Was there enough time for the interview?

b. How did the interview enhance the story?

c. How did the film help you understand the story?

(Worksheet 7.2—continued)

d. How did the film influence your opinion about the news story?

e. Was music used? How did the music influence your feelings?

5. Features

Summary of story:

a. Did the reporter's questions encourage the person interviewed to tell the story? Was there enough time for the interview?

b. How did the interview enhance the story?

c. How did the film help you understand the story? How did the film influence your opinion about the news story?

d. Was music used? How did the music influence your feelings?

6. General

Did you notice things during repeated viewings of the videotape newscast that were not apparent the first time you viewed the show? Name them.

Evaluation

Write a review of the newscast you watched. Rate it 1-5, with 1 the lowest and 5 the highest rating, based on the following.

- Time spent on each segment.
- Story presentation.
- Depth of the reports.
- Commercials
- Story selection.

(Worksheet 7.2—continued)

1. How much time was spent on each segment? Did the most important stories receive enough air time?

   Rating:

   Explain.

2. How well were the stories presented? Did interviews and pictures add to your understanding of the story? Did the reporter or anchor person give a clear explanation of the event?

   Rating:

   Explain.

3. Were the reports in-depth? Did some questions go unanswered?

   Rating:

   Explain.

4. Did commercials interfere with an important story?

   Rating:

   Explain.

5. Were there more entertainment stories than news stories?

   Rating:

   Explain.

6. Final rating:

7. Compare your evaluation of the newscast with other students' ratings. Discuss.

Worksheet 7.3: Comparing Television and Newspapers

Watching a newscast is very different from reading a newspaper. When we read a newspaper we can take our time to understand what we read. We can read editorials and think about the opinions expressed by the writers. Newspaper reporting offers greater depth and more detail than does television.

Television personalizes news. We can identify with the people involved, and the film allows us to enter worlds that we never could have witnessed before television. But because television is a visual medium, there is not much reporting of ideas. Pictures are exciting and dramatic, but they do not allow time for thought, and when they are presented in quick succession, the viewer is not able to absorb their meaning with any depth of understanding.

You were assigned to read a daily newspaper and to watch a newscast for the same day. You also watched a videotape of the newscast so that you could review in class what you saw at home. We are going to compare the way that television and newspapers handle the same or similar news stories.

QUESTIONS

1. Did both the newspaper and newscast have the same top story? If not, summarize each.

2. If the top stories are different, what do you think influenced the selection of the story?

3. Do you think that the most important story is always the top story in newspapers and on television? Explain.

4. How much time was devoted to the newscast's top story?

5. How long did it take you to read the newspaper's top story?

6. Which included more details?

7. Did any of the details differ in the newspaper and the newscast? If they did, what do you think was the reason?

8. Compare the impact of the photographs used in the newspaper with the film used on television.

9. Were interviews quoted in the newspaper? Were interviews aired or quoted on the newscast? How did the interviews compare?

10. Which presentation was more dramatic or exciting? What made it so?

(Worksheet 7.3—continued)

11. Did the drama or excitement help you understand the story? Explain.

12. Did the newscast give you enough information to understand the story?

13. Were there any opinions expressed in the newspaper article or the newscast? Explain.

14. Find and read three articles that appeared in the newspaper but not on the newscast. Should these stories have been included in the newscast? Why do you think they were not included?

15. How accurate is news reporting?

    Very Accurate   Sometimes Accurate   Never Accurate

    Explain.

16. Which is more accurate, television or newspapers? Explain.

17. Why do people still read newspapers if they can get the same information on television?

Worksheet 7.4: Information Networks

Computer technology is changing the way we find information. Everyone is familiar with newspapers and television, but not everyone is familiar with information networks. Networks provide information about news, the stock market, and the weather; they even let us shop without ever leaving home. Networks provide us with databases that give us information about any topic imaginable. They allow us to play games and to take quizzes for fun and recreation, and they allow us to join interest groups called forums. However, while newspapers and television are relatively inexpensive, information networks require a computer, modem, printer, software, and a subscription to an information network that charges hourly and monthly rates. Whether or not the vast information resources on a network are necessary depends on each individual's needs. For this project, you will access CompuServe, a commercial information network, and you will evaluate this source of information.

QUESTIONS

1. Name some of the ways in which technology touches our lives.

2. How do people get information through technology?

3. Do you know someone who uses an information network at home or at work? What kinds of information do they find?

INFORMATION NETWORKS

All information networks have the same basic features.

Forums allow people with similar interests to meet online to exchange information, ideas, and opinions. Forum subjects range from cooking and crafts to computers and world issues.

Electronic mail (E-mail) is used to send messages from the user of one computer to another. You can use a computer network to send and receive E-mail. All network users have a mailbox. When you send E-mail to someone, it is put in their personal mailbox. When you receive a message you may read it online or print it.

Computer bulletin boards are like large public mailboxes. Bulletin boards allow you to post messages for every user to read.

(Worksheet 7.4—continued)

USING COMPUSERVE

CompuServe is one of many large commercial information networks. CompuServe allows you to contact other users throughout the country and around the world. Many services are found on an information network such as CompuServe.

Travel information services allow you to get flight information, make a hotel reservation, find out about accommodations, and rent a car.

Shopping services allow you to order merchandise by computer.

Games on CompuServe range from adventure games to movie quizzes.

News services cover international, national, sports, entertainment, weather, business, and more.

Consumer Reports is a database that contains information about and ratings for various products. It is the electronic version of the magazine.

Reference material includes hundreds of databases offering information on a wide number of subjects. Databases are expensive to use.

Many of these services are costly. A plus sign (+) next to the name of a service when you are online means there is an additional fee for the use of this service; a dollar sign ($) indicates an even higher fee.

We will be using only those services included in the basic fee unless your teacher or librarian gives you permission to do otherwise.

Logon procedures differ with computers. Your librarian or teacher will give you the instructions you need to log on the service.

Worksheet 7.5: Using CompuServe

Use the logon procedures outlined for you by your teacher or librarian to access CompuServe. Be sure you understand how to save and print the information you find. The exercises on this worksheet will help you understand how to use the service and will help you become familiar with the kinds of information available. Keep in mind these exercises will show you only a small sample of what is available. Follow the instructions carefully and be sure to answer all the questions.

To begin, use the pull-down SERVICES menu, select GO and type INDEX. This will give you a list of CompuServe services with signs indicating whether each service is a basic service.

BASIC SERVICES

Basic Services are included in the monthly fee. There are no additional charges for these services.

1. Use the pull-down SERVICES menu, select GO and type BASIC SERVICES. From the BASIC SERVICES menu, select NEWS/WEATHER/SPORTS. From the NEWS/WEATHER/SPORTS menu, select ASSOCIATED PRESS ONLINE. From the ASSOCIATED PRESS ONLINE menu, select LATEST NEWS—UPDATED HOURLY. Read one article. Summarize the article.

2. Return to the ASSOCIATED PRESS ONLINE menu. Select FEATURE NEWS/TODAY IN HISTORY. Name one event that took place on this date in history.

3. Return to the ASSOCIATED PRESS ONLINE menu. Select WEATHER. Briefly describe the weather in your area for this date.

4. Return to the ASSOCIATED PRESS ONLINE menu. Select one other option. Briefly summarize what you found.

5. Close the ASSOCIATED PRESS ONLINE menu. Return to the BASIC SERVICES menu. From the BASIC SERVICES menu, select REFERENCE. From the REFERENCE menu select ACADEMIC AMERICAN ENCYCLOPEDIA.

   a. Make a copy of the introduction. Open the USER'S GUIDE menu. Open each option and save.

   b. Return to the ACADEMIC AMERICAN ENCYCLOPEDIA menu. Select SEARCH. Read the instructions carefully. Enter a search term.

   Search term:

   Write a short summary of the information you found, then save what you found.

6. Return to the ACADEMIC AMERICAN ENCYCLOPEDIA menu. Choose GROLIER'S BACKGROUND ON THE NEWS. Save and print.

Return to the BASIC SERVICES menu. Select one option, a feature that you usually enjoy reading in a newspaper or watching on television. Access this option and follow the directions. Save and print any information you would like to keep.

(Worksheet 7.5—continued)

7. From the SERVICES pull-down menu, select WHAT'S NEW. Find something of interest to you. Save and close the window. Print the file off-line.
8. From the SERVICES pull-down menu, select SPECIAL EVENTS. Find something of interest to you. Save and close the window. Print the file off-line.
9. From the SERVICES pull-down menu select FAVORITE PLACES. Play WHIZ QUIZ with a friend. Close the window.
10. At GO type CONSUMER REPORTS. Select HOW TO USE CONSUMER REPORTS. Select a product and access the product information. Save and print.

Keep experimenting with the Basic Services. It is a good way to learn how to use the network without incurring lots of expense. When you are experienced, and with your teacher's permission, you may use additional services.

MAIL

Use the MAIL pull-down menu to find any messages that were left in your mailbox.

1. If there is mail, write a reply. Make a copy of your reply and save it.
2. Write a message to a classmate and ask for a reply.

EXTENDED SERVICES

So far we have used only Basic Services. These services are included in the monthly rate that is charged by CompuServe. Other services on CompuServe require an hourly fee in addition to the monthly charge; these services should be accessed only with your teacher's permission. An extended service has a plus sign (+) after the name of the service. Services requiring additional fees are followed by a dollar sign ($).

These extended services include a wide range of forums. Forums allow people with similar interests to exchange information online. Each forum has a public bulletin board where messages are left for everyone to read. Each forum also has conferences in which you can speak to other forum members who are online at the same time you are. Each forum has a library. The library contains files left by other members of the forum.

STUDENT FORUM

To become familiar with the features of a forum, practice using STUDENT FORUM. Use the SERVICES pull-down menu, choose GO and type STUFO. This will bring you to the STUDENT FORUM.

1. Browse the messages. Read several that interest you and reply to one.
2. Try out the conference. See if someone is online. Start an online conversation.

(Worksheet 7.5—continued)

3. Finally, explore the library. Browse and, with your teacher's permission, download a file that interests you. Save it and print off-line.

INFORMATION USA

This extended service offers lots of free information about how to find information on a wide variety of subjects. Although Information USA is an extended service, much of the information it provides is free.

1. Use the pull-down SERVICES menu, and with your teacher's permission, type GO INFOUSA. Be sure to save the index and everything you access to print off-line.

IQUEST

Iquest is a collection of several hundred databases on innumerable subjects. Those followed by a dollar sign ($) have charges in addition to the monthly and hourly rates. Iquest should be used only if you have lots of experience using CompuServe, because this service can be quite costly.

CHARGES

Before disconnecting be sure to get a copy of the charges by typing GO CHARGES. The charges for the services you just accessed will not be available yet, but you will be able to get information about charges for earlier sessions.

The services that have been outlined are only a tiny fraction of what is available on a commercial information network. With your teacher's permission, experiment to find other services of interest to you.

Worksheet 7.6: Comparing and Evaluating Newspapers, Television, and Information Networks

Now that you have had the opportunity to get information from newspapers, television, and CompuServe, it's time to do some comparison shopping to evaluate which information source is best for various applications.

QUESTIONS

News Stories

Compare the news stories from CompuServe, the newscast, and the newspaper. Answer the following questions, giving reasons for your answers.

1. Which news story was the most understandable?
2. Which source gives the most up-to-date information?
3. Which offers the most complete information about current events?
4. Which is the easiest and most convenient to use?

Weather

1. Which source gave the most complete weather report?
2. If you had access to an information service like CompuServe, would you use it to find out about the weather? How do you usually find out about the weather?

Features

1. Which newspaper features or articles do you regularly read?
2. Were comparable features or articles available on CompuServe?
3. Were you able to access these features or articles through the Basic Services menu? If not, how costly were these features to access?

Reference

1. Using CompuServe did you find any information you wanted using any of the basic reference services, such as the encyclopedia or *Consumer Reports*?
2. Was the information of value?
3. How would you compare the value of the information and the ease of access with other reference sources you have used?

(Worksheet 7.6—continued)

Cost

1. How much did each group spend during its CompuServe session?
2. What was the total cost for all groups?
3. How much time did the class spend using CompuServe?

Evaluation

1. List the services the class accessed using CompuServe.
2. What information that you retrieved from CompuServe was most useful?
3. Was the most useful information also the most expensive?
4. Which source (television, newspaper, or CompuServe) gave the most value for the money spent?
5. Which was easiest to use?
6. Which was most enjoyable to use?
7. Which could you not live without?
8. Do they all serve the same purpose? Explain.
9. Every information source is particularly suited to deliver a certain kind of information. List the kinds of information best suited to each source given below.

   Newspapers:

   Television:

   CompuServe:

What's in a Name? Investigating the Past

A few years ago I realized that the school in which I worked was about to pass its seventy-fifth anniversary. I decided that a project involving the history of the school and the community would be perfect for a small group of gifted students. The school is located in an area of the Bronx in New York City with burned-out housing, dirty and depressing streets, and rampant drugs and violence. Most of the housing was nondescript; however, some homes were national landmarks. Indeed, many of the area's early settlers were prominent during and after the American Revolution, and at least one signed the Declaration of Independence. Through the years, the community had been home to a diverse immigrant population that had produced many notable people.

The students and I went to work. We placed ads in local newspapers, asking alumni to contact us. In old school records we made exciting discoveries, not the least of which was that General Colin Powell was one of our graduates. When General Powell became chairman of the Joint Chiefs of Staff, Rosemary Kerr's sixth grade class wrote to him. In return, General Powell invited a group of Rosemary's students to his Washington, D.C. office and even provided transportation.

Since then I have coordinated several local history projects, each one concentrating on a different aspect of the community's rich history. Students have always been enthusiastic participants.

Youngsters frequently believe that historic events are so remote, in both time and place, that they are meaningless and irrelevant. When students study the history of their communities, all history becomes concrete and personal, and they understand that history is happening all the time. Better understanding of the historical importance of their neighborhoods encourages pride in their community's past and optimism about their futures. There are dozens of ways to approach local history. The projects in this chapter concentrate on oral biographies and the use of technology to find information about ancestors. Table 8.1 gives a timetable for the projects in this chapter.

Students will interview elderly relatives and friends and visit nursing homes and senior centers to collect information from people who have first-hand knowledge of events. They will find out when various families settled in the area, why they chose to settle in the area, what members of the families did for a living, in what other places family members lived, which events of national and world importance took place during their lives, and how these events affected their lives. This investigation will encourage students to think about how historic events affect their own lives and will give students a new perspective on history. Interviewing enhances students' communication skills and helps to break down barriers between generations.

Alex Haley's *Roots* (the book and television miniseries) stirred enormous interest in family history. Tracing one's genealogy became popular; access to an electronic network enhances the search. With a network like CompuServe or America Online, students can join a genealogy forum to look for information about their own families and families prominent in their communities. During their research students will become aware of the importance of historical societies and national and state archives, and they will understand the importance of preserving historic documents.

Encyclopedias, both print and online, will be used for background information about events discussed during the interviews. A community and family history handbook, designed and written by the class, will be the final product. This handbook will provide information about local families, detailing their country of origin and dates of arrival in this country and in the community. The handbook also will feature family stories, traditions, and events that shaped family members' lives.

Bibliography

American Genealogical Research Institute Staff, *How to Trace Your Family Tree*. New York: Doubleday, 1973.

Table 8.1
Timetable for What's in a Name?

Project	Number of Library Periods	Number of Class Periods
Researching the Past		
Worksheet 8.1: History of the Community	2	4
Interviews		
Worksheet 8.2: Oral Biographies		4
Worksheet 8.3: Family History Form		2
Genealogy		
Worksheet 8.4: Family Trees	6 (per group)	
Worksheet 8.5: Finding Background Information About Historical Events	1 (per group) 3	2
Writing the Handbook		
Worksheet 8.6: The Handbook	2 6 (per group)	4
Total	7 +13 (per group)	16

Christianson, Betsy Pogue. *Interview Research: Make an Appointment with Success*. Buffalo, N.Y.: D.O.K., 1983.

Mabery, D. L. *Tell Me About Yourself*. New York: Lerner, 1985.

Zimmerman, William. *How to Tape Instant Oral Biographies*. New York: Guarionex, 1981.

Teaching Plan I: Researching the Past (Worksheet 8.1)

Materials: Background material about the community from the local historical society and state library.

Teaching Strategy: The class and teacher will determine the boundaries of the community they will study. A visit from a representative of the local historical society will provide the class with information to get started. The historian will show the students old photographs and slides of historic sites. In addition the state library will be asked to provide material in its archives. Historical maps will show how the community has changed. Census figures will provide information about the population. Local congressional offices and the offices of other officials may yield information about the community.

Teaching Plan II: Interviews (Worksheets 8.2 and 8.3)

Materials: Student notebooks.

Teaching Strategy: The teacher will discuss with the class why interviews are part of this project. The importance and validity of primary sources of information will be emphasized. Students will practice interviewing each other, learning to probe for information.

Students will interview an elderly relative, neighbor, or family friend. If possible, students will visit a nearby nursing home or senior center to interview elderly residents. Questions to be used for the interview appear on worksheet 8.2; students will develop additional questions. Questions should be specific; all documents that are shown during the interview should be carefully examined. Each student will record all information in a notebook. Family stories and traditions will be recorded in as much detail as possible.

All pertinent data will be recorded on worksheet 8.3, the family history form.* This form is very simple and can be used for only the briefest information. Multiple copies of the form will be made so that each person's history can be recorded on a separate form. For practice, students will fill out forms for themselves and members of their families before they begin the interviews.

*For more information about family history forms, contact Everton Publishers, P.O. Box 368, Logan, UT 84321; 800-443-6325; Family History Library, Church of the Latter Day Saints, 35 N.W. Temple St., Salt Lake City, UT 84150; National Genealogical Society, Educational Division, 4527 17th St., Arlington, VA 22207; or Smithsonian Institution Traveling Exhibition Service, Publications Department, Department 0564, Washington, DC 20073-0564 for their "Family Folklore Interviewing Guide and Questionnaire."

Teaching Plan III: Genealogy (Worksheets 8.4 and 8.5)

Materials: Completed interviews and family history forms; computer; modem; access to an information network, like CompuServe or America Online, with a genealogy forum.

Teaching Strategy: Students will begin with an understanding of the importance of primary documents, such as birth and marriage certificates. They will select a family name—their own, the name of someone close to them, the name of a person interviewed, or a name that is prominent in the city or town. Any student who uses the name of another person must obtain that person's permission, explaining that the research will be confined to public documents, such as military records and marriage certificates. Worksheet 8.3 will continue to be used as a means of recording each individual's history.

The teacher and librarian must be familiar with procedures for using the information network and the kinds of information available in the file libraries and message centers. The students will brainstorm about what information they are seeking. Students will receive instructions for accessing the information network and for downloading, saving, and printing.

Students will use the information from interviews and networks to understand how history affects ordinary people.

Teaching Plan IV: Writing the Handbook (Worksheet 8.6)

Materials: Information gathered from all sources: interviews, family history forms, background information about historical events, and information from the genealogy forums, including addresses of state archives; handbooks; computer; printer; software.

Teaching Strategy: Students will use the information they have gathered to write a handbook about the community. They will work in groups, with each group creating a different part of the handbook.

A variety of handbooks will be distributed to the class. The class will understand what a handbook is, the kinds of information it contains, and how it is used. The class will decide how to organize the handbook, what information to include, and whether to include photographs and copies of documents.

Copies of the completed handbook will be distributed to all participants as well as the local historical society.

Worksheet 8.1: History of the Community

A presentation by the local historical society will introduce you to the history of your community. You will use this information for a research project into the history of families living in your community.

QUESTIONS

Before the presentation answer the following questions.

1. Why do we need historical societies?
2. Where do historical societies get their material?
3. Why are old documents valuable?
4. Do you have anything that might be of interest to someone one hundred years from now? What?
5. How do you think this community has changed over the years?

During the presentation take notes about topics that you would like to know more about. Watch and listen carefully. Make only brief notes to help you remember what you want to ask after the presentation. After the presentation, use your notes to formulate the questions you want to ask. Use a separate sheet of paper for your notes.

FOLLOW-UP DISCUSSION

After the presentation and follow-up discussion, answer the following questions.

1. What information surprised you the most?
2. Have you ever visited any of the sites shown or discussed during the presentation? Which ones?
3. Which ones would you like to visit? Why?
4. How have lifestyles changed since the period shown or discussed?
5. Would you rather have lived then? Explain.
6. Have the lives of individuals improved since then? Explain.

(Worksheet 8.1—continued)

7. Additional comments.

Write a report about what you learned during the presentation. With your class, plan to visit some of the sites.

INFORMATION ABOUT THE COMMUNITY

Answer the following questions using information from the presentation or from other sources in the community and state.

1. When was your city founded?
2. Who helped found your community?
3. When did your community experience its largest growth in population?
4. What factors influenced the growth of your community?
5. Were any famous people born here?
6. When did the first immigrants arrive?
7. What countries did they come from?
8. Why did they leave their native lands?
9. What made them settle in this area of the country?
10. How has the ethnic or racial make-up of the community changed over the years?
11. Add any important additional information.

Worksheet 8.2: Oral Biographies

Every family and every community has a history that is important and worth hearing about. Memories can show us what life was like during an earlier time. History is not only battles and wars but events that affect individuals' lives. For this project you will interview your oldest relative or family friend. You will visit a senior center to interview its residents, and to listen to stories from people who have lived through events that you may have only read about. An interview is a way of obtaining information. When we speak to people who have lived through an event, and when we see old photos, documents, and mementos, the past becomes more vivid. Interviews provide us with a link to the future and an understanding that is not gained from textbooks.

HOW TO CONDUCT AN INTERVIEW

Make an appointment with the person you will interview. If you have never met the person, introduce yourself and explain the purpose of the interview. Show a genuine interest in the person.

Understand clearly what information you seek and your reasons for seeking this information. Tell the person that your class is gathering information for a community handbook that will contain information from the interview and from any old documents he or she might have.

Ask the person to show you some old photos, mementos, or documents that might help them remember events. Ask whether you may examine these materials to take notes. Explain that the class will use the computer to find additional information about family histories. Explain the kinds of information the class is looking for, such as country of origin, date of arrival in this country, occupation, and places their ancestors may have lived before coming to this community. If the person does not want you to do this, don't push it. Continue with the interview, gathering all the information you can. Explain that you are using family history forms to keep track of data like births and deaths.

Try to conduct the interview in a quiet place. If other people are around, they may join you later. Encourage the person you are interviewing by saying that something that seems unimportant might be very important. Sometimes the most important information comes when you least expect it. Listen carefully. Be patient and don't interrupt. Give the person enough time to answer each question. Be considerate of your subject's feelings and respect his or her right to refuse to answer a question. If you disagree with something the person says, don't show how you feel. Be polite! If you don't complete the interview, ask if you can return another time.

Take notes in a notebook. There will not be enough room on the interview sheet for all the answers. Don't worry about correct spelling or grammar when you are taking notes. You will rewrite the interview later. After the interview, write a letter to thank the individual.

TAPE RECORDING AN INTERVIEW

Ask for permission to use a tape recorder. Practice using the recorder before the interview to be sure you know how to use it. Bring along extra cassettes and batteries. Don't worry about pauses and incomplete sentences. You will rewrite the interview later.

(Worksheet 8.2—continued)

PROBING FOR ANSWERS

Sometimes people hesitate to give personal information. There are many ways to elicit complete answers.

Offer an experience of your own as an example that may help the person remember a forgotten event. For example, tell something about how your family celebrates birthdays to find out something more about the person's family traditions.

Ask the person to tell you more about an event that will help you gather additional personal information. Where was the person when World War II started? How did the war affect family life?

Ask the person to share a hobby or interest with you.

Ask the person to explain what he or she means when you feel a comment is important and needs elaboration.

Try to clarify replies that are vague. Ask specific questions. Use photos to jog the person's memory.

ROLE PLAYING

Practice interviewing in class. Work in pairs with each student taking turns interviewing and being interviewed. After the class has had practice, discuss interviewing techniques. Suggest possible changes or additions to the questions on the interview form.

Interview Form

Name of person being interviewed:

Sex:

Age:

QUESTIONS

Family History

1. Where were you born?
2. Who were the first members of your family to come to this country?
3. What country did they come from?
4. When did they come to this country?
5. Why did they leave their native land?
6. Where did they first settle?
7. What is your mother's maiden name?
8. What do you remember about your grandparents?
9. What did your father and grandfather do for a living?
10. Does this job still exist?
11. Did your mother or grandmother work outside the home?

Personal History

1. What are your earliest memories?
2. What is your saddest or happiest memory?
3. Can you share some family memories and traditions?
4. What chores were you expected to do when you were a child?
5. Describe your school life.
6. How much schooling do you have?

(Interview Form for Worksheet 8.2—continued)

7. What did you do for fun when you were a teenager or young adult?
8. What games did you play?
9. What were some of your friends names?
10. Are you still friendly with them?
11. Do you have any friends who might like to be included in this project?
12. How did you earn your living?
13. Tell me about your job. How much did you earn? What were the working conditions like?
14. Does this job still exist?
15. What were the most important personal events in your life? When did these take place?
16. May I examine any old documents you have about these events? (Marriage certificate; birth certificate; school records, such as diplomas; death certificates; religious records.)

Community History

1. How long have your lived in this neighborhood?
2. Describe this community as it was when you moved here.
3. Has it changed much? In what ways?
4. Tell us about the changes that you can remember.
5. How did these changes affect your life?
6. How have customs and lifestyles changed?
7. Do you think these changes are for the better?
8. How is life different now that it was when you were my age?
9. Can you share some stories that your family told about life in this community?

(Interview Form for Worksheet 8.2—continued)

World and National Events

1. What significant national or world events took place during your lifetime?
2. What effect did these events have on your life?
3. Did you serve in the armed forces of any country? What branch? Did you serve during a war?
4. Tell us something about your war experiences.
5. Did you live during a war without serving in the armed services?
6. What was life like at that time? Can you share some experiences with us?
7. Were there any hardships?
8. Did a member of your family ever serve in the armed forces?
9. Tell us what you know about those experiences.

Thank you very much for your time.

Worksheet 8.3: Family History Form

A separate form should be used for each individual. Complete the form as fully as possible.

Person's name: Date of birth:

Married to: Date of marriage:

Children and their dates of birth:

Father's name:

Place of birth: Date of birth:

Date of arrival in this community:

Died:

Occupation:

Schools attended:

Mother's name:

Place of birth: Date of birth:

Date of arrival in this community:

Died:

Occupation:

Schools attended:

Maternal grandmother's name:

Place of birth: Date of birth:

Date of arrival in this community:

Died:

Occupation:

Schools attended:

Maternal grandfather's name:

Place of birth: Date of birth:

Date of arrival in this community:

Died:

(Worksheet 8.3—continued)

Occupation:

Schools attended:

Paternal grandmother's name:

Place of birth: Date of birth:

Date of arrival in this community:

Died:

Occupation:

Schools attended:

Paternal grandfather's name:

Place of birth: Date of birth:

Date of arrival in this community:

Died:

Occupation:

Schools attended:

Names of first relatives to come to this country:

Dates of arrival:

Countries of origin:

Religion:

Military service:

Branch of military:

In what country?

When?

Worksheet 8.4: Family Trees

Genealogy is the study of families and their history. It has become popular in the decade since the broadcast of *Roots*, the miniseries about the author's search for his African origins, based on the book of the same name by Alex Haley.

Genealogists use documents like birth and marriage certificates, census records, and religious records to learn about a family's ancestors. They may even go to old tombstones to learn about ancestors! We are going to trace families through documents using the information you obtained from your interviews and information you will obtain through information networks that have forums and clubs that help people trace family histories. You are going to access an information network to find additional information abut the family you are researching as well as information about where to look for such information.

In an information network a forum is a "meeting place" for users with similar interests. Forums allow users to exchange information, ideas, and opinions. For this project you will use the genealogy forum on whatever information network is available in your library media center. Most forums offer three features: a mail or message center, conferences, and a library of documents available to everyone. Networks may call these services by various names, but their functions are the same.

Message centers allow forum members to leave E-mail, make inquiries, or answer a question posed by another member. Browsing through the message center is a good way to find information. You can use the message center to ask other users to help you find the information you need.

Conferences are online meetings. During a conference you can communicate with other forum members online. Watch for notices about scheduled conferences. Sometimes experts are available online for a conference. People who belong to online forums are very helpful; if possible you should join in conferences.

Libraries are storehouses of files. People upload, or leave, files on the system. You can download, or copy, these files onto your hard drive or floppy disk. Most genealogy forums have lots of files to retrieve. With your teacher's permission, find files that are of interest to others in the class. Download the files, print off-line, and distribute copies to classmates who need them. Be sure you understand how to download using your telecommunications software and the information network.

When you access the forum you will find loads of information. It's important to save or download what is needed, but you do not need to save everything you find. Be sure to record names and addresses of state and national libraries and archives. Print off-line after you exit the network.

FAMILY RESEARCH

You have interviewed a relative, or someone close to you, and one other elderly person for this project. You may use your own family, or the family of a person close to you, or you may use the family of the person you interviewed *if that person gave you permission to do so.*

Professional genealogists use complicated charts and computer software to analyze the results of their search. We will continue to use the family history form (see worksheet 8.3). Remember, data for each family member is to be recorded on a separate form.

(Worksheet 8.4—continued)

The following will help you prepare to go online.

Family name:

Circle the documents you already have:

Birth Certificates Marriage Certificates Death Certificates Military Records

Records of Citizenship Baptismal Records School Records Other

Be sure you have recorded all the information you already have on the family history form. Be sure to complete a form for each individual.

Worksheet 8.5: Finding Background Information About Historical Events

You have now completed both your oral biographies and family history forms. You have lots of information about your family or people close to you and some people who live in your community. People have told you family stories and have talked about events that took place during their lives. Now you need to obtain background information about the events. This information can be found using a print or online encyclopedia, or you can search the library catalog to find history books. Each information network may offer a different online encyclopedia, but the search techniques are the same for all. When using online encyclopedias it's best to use broad search terms. This allows you to narrow the topic based on the list of articles you find.

You are going to find information about events that the people you interviewed considered significant. You will need background information about the significant events. These events may have changed your subjects' lives and the lives of others in the community. The events can be the circumstances that brought families to this country, such as wars, famines, revolutions, the Great Depression, or the invention of a product that changed the occupation of a person or the industry of a community. In addition to events of personal importance, you will research factors that contributed to the growth of the community. These factors may overlap with events of personal importance.

QUESTIONS

1. What was the most significant historical event in the lifetime of the person you interviewed?
2. What made this person's family immigrate to the United States?
3. Why did the family choose to settle in your community? Was the area similar to the area the family left in its native land? If so, describe the similar geographical details.
4. What historic events occurred in the period of history during which your community experienced the greatest growth?
5. What kinds of employment were prevalent in this community in various time periods, and what factors caused them to change?
6. Describe factors of urbanization or industrial growth that may have affected the community.
7. Has the racial and ethnic population changed over the years? What factors led to that change?
8. Describe how national events may have affected the community's growth.

Make a time line showing the national events, inventions, and industrial development that changed your community. Include any other happenings of importance to your community.

Worksheet 8.6: The Handbook

A handbook is a small reference book with lots of brief, varied information about a particular subject. Some handbooks are instruction manuals or guides to information about jobs and hobbies. Some handbooks provide information that is difficult to find elsewhere. Your class is going to design and write a handbook about your community and about the families who live there now or may have lived there in the past. You will use the information you have gathered from all your research: the interviews, family history forms, the genealogy forum, the presentation given by the historical society, books, information you received from other organizations or libraries, and any information about the events that people felt were important to their lives.

WRITING THE HANDBOOK

Because you have notebooks filled with lots of interesting and important information, you must decide how to organize the handbook and what information to include. Ask yourself

- Who is the intended audience?
- Should the handbook include copies of old photographs, letters, and documents?
- Should the handbook display statistical information graphically? For example, should data about population changes be converted into a chart or graph?
- Should the handbook include a list of historical societies, genealogical societies, and state libraries and archives?
- How should the handbook be organized?

PARTS OF THE HANDBOOK

Work in groups, with each group responsible for a different part of the book. The parts of the handbook and the way you organize it will depend to some extent on the community you are writing about. Include some or all of the following:

Introduction. Why did you undertake this big project, and what did you learn from it?

Historical background about the community. When was the community founded? Who were the first settlers? Where did they come from and why?

Historical sites. Where are local historical sites? When were they built? What is their significance?

Families. Write the interviews as narratives. This will probably be the most interesting and informative part of your handbook. The oral biographies are primary source material, and they are invaluable. Be sure to include such things as family traditions, school and lifestyle changes, and all the personal history you recorded. If photographs and documents are to be used, be sure to obtain the permission of the people involved. Information from the family history forms and genealogy forums should be included here.

Urbanization and population changes. How and why has the racial and ethnic population changed? What technological changes, such as transportation, communications, and industrialization, caused changes to occur?

(Worksheet 8.6—continued)

Economic changes. How have the ways people earn their living changed? How has this changed the community?

Historical events. Which national and world events had the greatest effect on lives of your interviewees and their families? Be sure to include background data on both national and local levels. For example, how many people from the community served in the Vietnam War? Were any of them killed in action?

Places to contact for further information. People reading your handbook may want to find out more about their families. Tell them about national and state archives and libraries as well as the information network you used for the genealogy forum.

Time line. Graphically show how various changes and events have affected the community.

Thank you. Be sure to thank all the people you interviewed, the representative from the historical society, and anyone else who helped you.

PRINTING THE HANDBOOK

Use desktop publishing software to lay out and print the handbook. Make many copies on a photocopier, and bind them with staples or a binder. Distribute the handbook to parent groups, local historical societies, and each person interviewed.

Taking a Trip Via a Telecommunication Network

Everyone loves an adventure, traveling to unexplored territory, not knowing what or who will be encountered along the way or at the destination. Taking an imaginary trip and using a computer to write about it, although not as exciting as the real thing, can stimulate interest in geography and history. Pen pals are nothing new; writing to someone far away has always been popular with students and teachers. Using a computer to send and receive mail lends new excitement; it is no wonder that telecommunicating with a partner class in another city has become such a popular activity.

NYCENET, the New York City Educational Network, is one of many networks that coordinates partner classes both nationally and internationally.

The problem sometimes encountered with these programs is certainly not lack of enthusiasm but lack of planning. Without planning, a telecommunications program is doomed. Having a precise plan and timetable helps to reduce frustration and the likelihood that one or both classes will drop out before completing the exchange. This chapter provides a plan for one such exchange. Table 9.1 gives a timetable for the projects outlined in this chapter.

Note that the instructions are written as if students were really traveling; they are said to visit or stay in places. This language is used to simplify the instructions; it does not imply that the trip is meant to be taken.

Students will telecommunicate with a partner class and will plan a trip to visit that class. Each class will select a route to follow and will learn about the people, geographic features, and historic landmarks of selected stops on the way to their destination. Each class will produce a map that shows the route the class will travel to the city in which the other class is located. (For books about how to use maps, see the bibliography on p. 131.)

In each class students will discuss the kinds of places they would like to visit; everything from camping at a national park to a visit to a presidential library is acceptable. Groups will be formed based on students' interests. Each group will select one place to visit, or research, and will write a report about its visit. Groups from one class will exchange reports with similar groups in the partner class. The groups will evaluate each other's work.

Students will request brochures from travel bureaus and chambers of commerce; they will use atlases, almanacs, and travel books to get additional information about the places their groups will visit. All of the groups in both classes will contribute to a travel brochure that highlights all of the visits the groups made.

In addition to group and class exchanges, some students will telecommunicate with an "E-mail pal" in the partner class. The teachers will match students based on similar interests.

The teacher or librarian will begin by introducing the class to telecommunication networks. Students will become familiar with the vocabulary of telecommunications and with the procedures for using a network. They will practice sending each other messages before sending messages to the partner class. Before going online they should understand the functions of forums, electronic mail, and bulletin boards, and they should be familiar with uploading and downloading procedures.

Students will use map skills as they think about the route of their trip. Each class will use critical thinking skills as they decide which places to visit, what to see when they get there, and how long to stay at the group's stop on the way to the destination. They will use almanacs to find factual information about the sites and travel books, magazines, and newspaper articles for the specific information necessary (e.g., weather) to make the group's stop enjoyable.

Students will mark each group's stops along the route to the destination. Students may even pretend to meet people at their stop based on their research about the people who live in the places they are visiting. All of this information will be exchanged with the partner class. Each group in each class will write about one stop only; the number of stops will depend on the number of groups in the classes. Each group will be paired with a partner group. When each class arrives at its final

Table 9.1
Timetable for Taking a Trip

Project	Number of Library Periods	Number of Class Periods
Telecommunication Networks		
Worksheet 9.1: Telecommunication Networks	1	
	2 (per group)	
Worksheet 9.2: Student Questionnaire		
Individual online exchanges*		1
Planning the Itinerary		
Worksheet 9.3: Map Skills		
Online exchange** (1 group only)	4	
Worksheet 9.4: The Itinerary	1	4
Online exchange	1 (per group)	
Finding Travel Information		
Worksheet 9.5: The Almanac	1	
Worksheet 9.6: Travel Information	4 (per group)	
Online exchange	1 (per group)	
We Have Arrived!		
Worksheet 9.7: We Have Arrived!		4
Online exchange	2 (per group)	
Worksheet 9.8: The Travel Brochure		4
Online exchange	1 (per group)	
Printing the brochure	2 (per group)	
Total	7	13
	+8 (per group)	
Online exchanges	+6 (per group)	

*Exchanges between individual students should be an ongoing activity as time permits.

**Online exchange worksheet 9.3, 1 group of selected students only.

destination, it would be nice to prepare a welcoming party and show the guests around the city.

After each group has visited its stop, it should write a narrative about where it has been, what students saw, and whether the place lived up to their expectations. This narrative should be sent to the partner class for evaluation, then copied and distributed to the other groups in the class.

The information exchanged by the classes will be used to develop a travel brochure to be shared with other classes, teachers, and administrators.

Bibliography

Carey, Helen. *How to Use Maps and Globes*. New York: Franklin Watts, 1983.

Lambert, David. *Maps and Globes*. Bookwright Press, 1987.

Weiss, Harvey. *Maps: Getting from Here to There*. Boston: Houghton Mifflin, 1991.

Teaching Plan I: Telecommunication Networks (Worksheets 9.1 and 9.2)

Materials: Access to a telecommunications network that provides a partnership program with a class at a distant location, computer, modem, telecommunications software.

Teaching Strategy: Using worksheet 9.1 students will become familiar with the terminology of computers and networks and the protocols for the network they will be using. Students will practice all procedures. Worksheet 9.1 provides exercises.

Before the class begins communicating with its partner class, each student will fill out the questionnaire on worksheet 9.2. The class will discuss the questions to include or eliminate and suggest additional questions. If possible teachers at both locations will pair students with similar interests and let them start to exchange messages. This exchange will continue throughout the project.

Teaching Plan II: Planning the Itinerary (Worksheets 9.3 and 9.4)

Materials: Class set of maps showing the destination and origination sites and all points between them, computer, modem, word processing software, telecommunications software.

Teaching Strategy: This project emphasizes map skills. Worksheet 9.3 emphasizes the language and use of maps. Students will begin this project in the library after they have had some practice using maps and atlases in class.

Students will practice using maps to locate their city and to describe geographical features of the area in which they live. All students will use a copy of the same map, large enough to show both the origination and destination cities, if possible. The information about geographical features will be transmitted to the partner class as the first class exchange. A group of students selected by the teacher will be responsible for this exchange. These students will print the information received during the exchange, make copies and distribute to the class. Next students will think about the places, between their city and the destination city, that they would like to visit. Groups will be formed based on shared interests. These groups will be paired with groups of similar interests in the partner class. Using Worksheet 9.4 the class will develop an itinerary indicating each stop on the trip. Each group will visit only one stop. This itinerary will be exchanged with the partner class.

Teaching Plan III: Finding Travel Information (Worksheets 9.5 and 9.6)

Materials: Almanacs, travel books and magazines, brochures from travel agencies and chambers of commerce, travel sections of newspapers, books that provide historical information about the travel destination, computer, word processing software, telecommunications software, modem.

Teaching Strategy: Students will use the almanac to find facts about the places they will be visiting. They will look for information using books, periodicals, newspapers, and brochures from chambers of commerce and travel agencies.

Each group will discuss in detail the practical answers to everyday travel questions that they need. Worksheet 9.6 suggests questions that must be answered in preparation for a successful and enjoyable journey.

Each group will leave from the stop visited by the previous group and will journey to its stop. All relevant newspaper and magazine articles located in the school library media center should be clipped and saved, because each group will do its research when the previous group is finished.

Teaching Plan IV: We Have Arrived! (Worksheets 9.7 and 9.8)

Materials: All information gathered by all the groups, plans for the trip, word processing software, desktop publishing software, computer, modem, telecommunications software, printer.

Teaching Strategy: At this time all the groups have completed their research and arrived at their stop. Now they will begin to write a group or individual narrative describing the visit. The narrative may describe people and events that are imaginary, but must be based on the research. This narrative will be uploaded to the partner group and copies will be distributed to all groups in the same class. The partner group will evaluate the information and communicate its suggestions for additional information.

Each group will go from their stop to the destination city and "meet" there when all the research has been completed. The host class will prepare a welcome party for their visitors, taking them to see landmarks or places of interest and giving them information about the city. Partner class members will write about how they feel about the place and the welcome they received. Students who have been corresponding individually by electronic mail will write individual responses. If possible, the classes will exchange photos by postal mail.

The final activity and worksheet is the travel brochure. Students from both classes will design an illustrated brochure, writing about their stops and destination in glowing terms. They will use desktop publishing software to produce the brochure. One brochure with contributions from both classes is the final outcome. The teachers will select the material to appear in the brochure. Narratives about the stops and the destination cities will be included in the brochure.

Worksheet 9.1: Telecommunication Networks

A communications network links computers at various locations. Although the procedures for using a network may differ according to the network protocols and your telecommunications software, all networks offer some features in common. Electronic mail or E-mail allows you to send and receive private messages. It serves as a private mailbox. Bulletin boards serve as message centers. Users can post messages that are meant to be read by everyone. When you read an interesting message, you may then leave a message in reply; you may receive many messages in reply. A message and all its replies is called a thread. Forums allow you to communicate with people with similar interests. Many networks have student forums; using these forums you can communicate with other students at many different locations.

GLOSSARY: NETWORKS

Downloading. Copying files from the network onto a hard drive or floppy disk. Downloading allows you to read or print the file off-line. Because network and telecommunications charges are based on how long you are logged on, downloading helps to cut the cost of using a network. Procedures for downloading vary depending on the network and telecommunications software you are using.

File library. A collection of files that have been uploaded to the network computer. A network might have several libraries, each devoted to a different topic or forum. Users search a library to find information they might want to download.

Logon and logoff procedures. Logging on is accessing a network, logging off is exiting the network. Logon and logoff procedures are the steps taken to access and exit. These procedures vary from one network to another.

Menu. A list of options. Many menus are available on a network. Menus may offer functional options, such as Save or Delete, or they may offer feature options, such as the names of forums or databases.

Modem. A device used to transmit data over telephone lines.

Password. A secret code that allows the network administrators and software to identify you. On most networks you must enter your password as part of the logon procedure. Each student may have an individual password and mailbox, or there may be only one password and mailbox for the entire class. Usually the user—whether an individual or a group—may select the password to be used. If you have your own password, make it easy to remember and keep it secret.

Telecommunications software. Software that allows the computer user to send and receive information over telephone lines. There are many kinds of telecommunications software.

Uploading. Sending a file to another location, which is actually saving a file to a disk (hard drive or floppy disk) at a remote computer. When you upload files to the network, you are saving those files on the network's drive. When you upload files directly to a friend's computer, you can set it up to save to that person's hard drive or floppy disk. You may upload long or short files. You can use word processing software, such as MacWrite or WordPerfect, to write the message or file, and then upload it using the procedures dictated by your network and telecommunications software.

(Worksheet 9.1—continued)

QUESTIONS

1. Which software is used in your school media center?
2. What modem is used in your media center?
3. What network will you be using?
   Logon procedure:
   Logoff procedure:
4. Logon to your network. Name some of the choices available at the main menu.
5. Name the steps to use for downloading files from the network you are using.
6. Name the steps to use for uploading a file to the network you are using.

USING THE NETWORK

Before going online with your partner class, it is important to practice all telecommunicating procedures. Some networks limit the amount of time you may be online, so think about what you want to say and write your messages before you go online. The exercises on this worksheet will help you become comfortable with telecommunicating.

Mail

Compose a message describing yourself. Send the message to a classmate's mailbox, but don't sign it. When you receive an unsigned message, guess who sent it and send a reply.

Write the opening sentence of a story. Send it to a classmate's mailbox. Your classmate will write a short paragraph to continue the story and then send it to another classmate until all the students in the class have contributed to the story.

File Library

Browse through a network library. When you find a file that looks interesting, download it, make copies, and share it with your class.

Practice uploading by sending a file to a network library.

Forums

Browse the student forum on your network, if it has one, and read some of the messages that have been left there. Start a new thread or reply to a message. Return one week later to see if anyone has written to you.

Worksheet 9.2: Student Questionnaire

Read through the following questionnaire and then participate in a class discussion about it. The purpose of the questionnaire is to let a student in your partner class get to know you. Suggest ways to improve the questionnaire by adding or dropping questions.

Answer the questions in narrative form using full sentences. Use the computer to exchange completed questionnaires with your partner class. If possible, you will be paired with a student with similar interests. During the course of this project, exchange personal messages with your E-mail pal in addition to completing your group assignments.

Name:

Age: Grade: School:

Address:

City: State: Zip:

QUESTIONS

1. Do you live in a city, suburb, or rural community?
2. What do you like to do in your spare time?
3. What is your best friend's name?
4. What do you like to do together?
5. What are your favorite school subjects?
6. What are your least favorite subjects?
7. What things do you hate about school?
8. What kind of music do you like? What is your favorite group?
9. What is your favorite television show?
10. What do you want to be when you finish school?
11. What do you think is the most serious world or national problem? Why?
12. What places have you visited?
13. What places would you like to visit if you could?

Worksheet 9.3: Map Skills

For this project you will take an imaginary trip to a distant city, and you will exchange information about the places you visit along the way with a class at the destination city. You will send your partner class information about the geography of the area in which you live, and you will receive the same kind of information about the destination city from your partner class. Your school and public libraries have many atlases that can be used for this project.

USING ATLASES

An atlas is a book of maps that also includes geographic information and statistics in the form of graphs and tables. The index helps you find information about various places. Using the atlas in your school library or classroom, answer as many of the following questions as you can.

1. What is the population of your city?
2. What is the average temperature in your area?
   Average summer temperature? Average winter temperature?
3. What is the average rainfall per year?
4. What is the average snowfall per year?
5. Do hurricanes, tornadoes, or floods ever occur in your area?
6. What clothing should be worn in your city at this time of year?
7. In what time zone is your city located?
8. What additional information will help your partner class prepare for this trip? (For example, are there good hiking trails or important historical sites nearby?)

GLOSSARY: MAP TERMS

Compass rose. A symbol that indicates north on a map. The longest petals (or pointers) point north, south, east, and west. Shorter petals indicate, for example, northwest or southeast. Most compass roses look more like a cross than a flower.

General reference map. Map that shows natural features, such as mountains, lakes, rivers, oceans, the size and location of cities and towns; and other important features, such as historical sites, recreational sites, and facilities such as airports.

Key or legend. Usually located at a bottom corner of the map, the key or legend defines the symbols used on the map.

Latitude. Imaginary lines or parallels on a map that show how far north or south of the equator a place is. Latitude is measured in degrees. A point on the equator has a latitude of 0 degrees. The North Pole has a latitude of 90 degrees north. The South Pole has a latitude of 90 degrees south.

(Worksheet 9.3—continued)

Longitude. The measure of distance of any point east or west of the imaginary line running from the North Pole to the South Pole through Greenwich, England. Longitude is measured in degrees. Greenwich is at 0 degrees. Latitude and longitude are the two coordinates that locate a place on Earth.

Map index. An alphabetical list of all the places on a map with a location key to help you find the place on the map.

Political map. A map that shows the boundaries and locations of countries and their subdivisions, such as provinces or states. Detailed political maps may show congressional districts, counties, or even voting precincts.

Road map. A general reference map that also shows expressways, highways, and roads.

Scale. A map's scale indicates how many miles per inch are represented on the map. A large scale map covers a small area and shows many details. A small scale map covers a large area but omits many details.

Thematic map. A map marked to provide information about the world's land, people, and cultures.

Topographical map. A map that shows the location and elevation of natural features, such as lakes and mountains. Many topographic maps also show manmade features, such as roads and trails.

USING MAPS

Use a general reference map to answer the following questions.

1. What are the location keys (see definition of *map index* in the Glossary above) for your city and for the destination city?
2. Measure the shortest route between your city and the destination city.
3. Using this route what states must you cross?
4. Name any mountain ranges or rivers along this route.
5. What is the latitude and longitude of the city in which you live?
6. Name the geographical features in the area in which you live. Give the map symbol used for each feature.

   Mountain ranges: Rivers: Ocean:

   Lakes: Other:

7. What is the capital of your state?
8. What is the map symbol for state capitals?

Your teacher or librarian will select a group of students to exchange this geographic information with your partner class.

Worksheet 9.4: The Itinerary

You have started to exchange information about your city with your partner class, and perhaps some of you have been using the computer to send E-mail to your new friends. You have identified a route to take to visit your partner class. Now it is time to decide where you will stop on the way to your destination. To incorporate all the stops classmates wish to make, it may be necessary to use a longer route than the class planned. As a class you must decide if a detour is worth the extra time.

As a class, discuss the kinds of places you would enjoy visiting. Join with three or four students who want to visit the same place you want to visit. Your group will research one stop. Answer the following questions to help you decide which place you would most like to visit on the trip to visit your partner class. Remember, you can visit only one place on this trip.

QUESTIONS

National Park

1. Is there a national park on the route to the destination city? Is a detour necessary?
2. Name the park.
3. In what state is it located?
4. Which states must you cross to get there?
5. How far is it from your destination?
6. Do you want to visit this national park on this trip?

Large City

1. Are there large cities on the route? Is a detour necessary?
2. Do you want to visit any monuments, museums, sports arenas, or historic sites in any of these cities?
3. Name the place you would like to visit.
4. Name the city in which this place is located.
5. In what state is this city located?
6. What states must you cross to get there?
7. How far is it from your destination?
8. Do you want to visit a large city on this trip?

Mountain Range

1. Is there a mountain range on the route? Is a detour necessary?
2. Name the mountain range.
3. In what state is the part of the range that you would like to visit?
4. What states must you cross to get there?

(Worksheet 9.4—continued)

5. How far is it from your destination?

6. Will you be camping out there?

7. Do you want to visit a mountain range on this trip?

Lake, River, or Ocean

1. Is there a body of water on the route or at your destination? Is a detour necessary?

2. Name the body of water that you would like to visit.

3. In what state is it located?

4. What states must you cross to get there?

5. How far is it from your destination?

6. What will you do there?

7. Do you want to visit a body of water on this trip?

Museum or Historic Site

1. Is there a museum or historic site on the route? Is a detour necessary?

2. Name the museum or historic site you would like to visit.

3. In what state is it located?

4. What states must you cross to get there?

5. How far is it from your destination?

6. Do you want to visit this site on this trip?

Special Interest

1. Is there a place of special interest on the route or at your destination? If so, what is it?

2. Is a detour necessary?

3. In what state is it located?

4. What states must you cross to get there?

5. How far is it from your destination?

6. Do you want to visit this site?

Historic Person

1. Is there a home or library of a historic person on the route or at your destination? Is a detour necessary?

2. Name the home or library that you would like to visit.

3. In what state is this home or library located?

(Worksheet 9.4—continued)

4. What states must you cross to get there?
5. How far is it from your destination?
6. Do you want to visit this site on this trip?

Other

1. Is there a place not mentioned that you would like to visit?
2. Is the place on the route? Is a detour necessary?
3. Name the place.
4. In what state is it located?
5. What states must you cross to get there?
6. How far is it from your destination?
7. Do you want to visit this place on this trip?

THE ITINERARY

Name the places the class will visit. Use your map to identify the order of the stops. Plan your route to minimize backtracking and detours.

Group 1—first stop:

Group 2—second stop:

Group 3—third stop:

Group 4—fourth stop:

Group 5—fifth stop:

Each group of students will research one stop. Groups will take turns using the library for research, starting with the first group.

Each group will leave for its stop from the previous stop. For example, group 1 travels from home to stop one, group 2 travels from stop one to stop two, and so forth. The last group will go from its stop to the destination.

MAKING A MAP OF THE TRIP

Your class will make a map of the route of the trip from start to finish, including all stops. Your partner class will make a similar map for the trip it is planning. Your maps may be different; the other class might choose a different route or might make different stops. If possible your group will be teamed with a partner group that is visiting the same place that your group is visiting.

Prepare your class map. Mark each stop "Stop 1, Stop 2," and so forth. Make a list of the names of members of each group. Exchange maps and lists by postal mail with your partner class.

(Worksheet 9.4—continued)

QUESTIONS

Answer the following questions about your class's map.

1. What is the longitude and latitude of the stop your group is researching?
2. In what time zone is your stop located?
3. What is the distance between each stop?
4. What is the distance between your stop and your home?
5. What is the distance between your stop and the previous one?
6. What is the distance between your stop and the destination?
7. Name the states you will cross to get from your home to your stop.
8. Name any geographical features, such as rivers, lakes, or mountains, that you must cross to get from home to your stop.
9. What states and time zones, if any, do you cross to get from the previous stop to your stop?

Worksheet 9.5: The Almanac

An almanac gives short, concise information about many subjects. It is a good place to find facts about the place you will visit on your trip. Almanacs are published each year and information provided is for the previous year. For example, the 1992 almanac provides information about people, places, and events that took place in 1991.

Although almanacs provide much of the same information, each is arranged a little differently. Browse through the almanac to become familiar with its arrangement.

QUESTIONS: USING THE ALMANAC

1. Name and number of your group's stop on itinerary.
2. In what state is your stop located?
3. Using the table of contents or the index, find the answers to the following questions.
   a. What is the state capital?
   b. What is the state symbol and nickname?
   c. How did the state get its name?
   d. What is the population and racial or ethnic makeup of the state?
   e. What are the largest cities in the state?
   f. If you are visiting a city, is it listed as one of the largest cities in the state?
   g. Is your stop listed as a major point of interest?
   h. What are some of the other points of interest?
4. Does the almanac provide other interesting information about this state or the place you are visiting? Summarize.
5. Find the address of a chamber of commerce and write for information about your stop.
6. What information about your stop will be useful on your trip?
7. Browse through the index and table of contents to find other listings for your stop. Note anything of interest.

Worksheet 9.6: Travel Information

Now you will begin to use many research sources to find information about the place your group will visit.

CHAMBERS OF COMMERCE

Write to the local chamber of commerce for information about your stop. Ask for a map of the area. In the space provided here, copy the chamber of commerce address from the almanac.

____

____

____

TELEPHONE NUMBERS

Call the toll-free information operator at 1-800-555-1212 and ask for visitor information centers, travel bureaus, or any travel listings for your stop. If no local chamber of commerce address was in the almanac, see if there is a toll-free telephone number for it. Copy the telephone numbers here.

Telephone numbers:

NEWSPAPERS

Scan your newspaper's travel section to see if your stop is featured. Clip and save the article. Note any information you may need, such as where to stay, how to get there, special places to visit, and prices of admission to places of interest.

TRAVEL AGENCIES

If there is a travel agency in your area, or if there is a listing for one in the yellow pages directory under travel, call or write to ask for brochures about your stop.

Travel agencies:

TRAVEL BOOKS AND MAGAZINES

Don't forget to use the catalog in your school and public libraries to find books loaded with travel information.

Find out which travel magazines are available in your local and school libraries. Ask teachers, family members, and friends for copies of travel magazines they receive.

(Worksheet 9.6—continued)

FRIENDS AND RELATIVES

Often the best travel information comes from someone who has been there. Ask your friends and relatives not only about your stop, but all the stops being made and see if any one has been to these places and can give you advice to pass along to the other groups.

WHAT INFORMATION DO WE NEED?

To plan a successful trip, you should get lots of information before you leave. Brainstorm with your group about the kinds of information you will need. Each group may stop at a different kind of place: some may be going camping, others may visit a big city or a historic site. Each group may need to take different kinds of things. One thing you will need, whether you visit a large city or a wilderness area, is a large-scale map of the area. This may be available from the local chamber of commerce, or from a travel agent, or in travel books.

Use the following suggestions as a guide in deciding what information your group needs to collect. Each person in the group may be responsible for a different category of information.

Organize your information by topic on 5-by-7-inch index cards.

Accommodations

Where are we staying? How long? What will it cost?

Weather

What time of the year are we traveling? Is there a chance that we might encounter some rough weather? What kinds of clothing should we pack?

Equipment

Is there any special equipment we will need for this trip?

Activities

What are we going to do once we get there? Are we going to stay together for the entire stop, or will we split up to visit different places at the stop?

Food

Where are we going to eat? How much do we want to spend on food?

WE'RE OFF!

Okay, we're on our way! Type all the information from the index cards onto the computer using word processing software. Upload the file to the partner class. They will do the same, and you will download their work.

Worksheet 9.7: We Have Arrived!

You have finally arrived at your stop.

ABOUT THE STOP

You have a great deal of information about the place you visited. These are some of the questions to think about as you write about your stop. Some of them will require you to use your imagination based on your research.

- Did your research prepare you well? Did you have enough information? Which travel resource was the most useful?
- Did your visit meet all your expectations? Were you disappointed in anything?
- Did you encounter any bad weather? Were you prepared for it?
- Describe your accommodations. Did you meet any interesting people? Describe them and the circumstances under which you met them. Did they invite you to their homes? Describe where and how they live.
- Describe some of the landmarks, historic sites, or other places of interest. Describe the activities you took part in while on your visit.

WELCOME YOUR GUESTS

Your friends have arrived! Plan to welcome them with a party that features local food and entertainment. Show your friends some local landmarks and explain their significance. Have your friends "meet" some interesting people who live in your town. Tell your friends about the history of your town. If your town or city is situated at or near a special geographical feature, describe it and explain how the geography has influenced the way people work and play.

REACTIONS TO THE DESTINATION

The trip is over, you have met your new friends and visited their town. They gave a swell party. You met all kinds of new people, many from different ethnic backgrounds, and you ate unusual foods. What do you think of it all?

Worksheet 9.8: The Travel Brochure

A travel brochure is a small booklet that provides information about a particular place. In doing research for this project, you may have used such brochures to find information. We are going to design, write, and print a travel brochure about the destination cities and all of the places you and your partner class visited on your trips. Remember that you are selling these places; don't write anything negative. This is a good opportunity to use the thesaurus to find glowing words to describe the trip.

Include some or all of the following in your brochure.

Cover. An attractively illustrated cover will entice readers. The cover should give clues about what is inside.

Table of contents. This will let your readers know what is included in the brochure and where to find what they are looking for.

Introduction. Each group should write a description of the project, telling readers what the trip was about and why particular stops were selected. The introduction should entice the reader to want to know more about the stops. What special something made your group pick its stop?

Location. A map of the route, with all the stops marked, should be included. Each group should describe the location of their stop. Also include the mileage from one stop to the next, time zones, and travel information.

Climate. The weather should be described in glowing terms. If it snows or rains a lot, describe what can be done on rainy or snowy days to make this an enjoyable visit.

Scenery. All geographic features should be described in breathtaking detail. Include details that make the place special.

Special attractions. Is this area known for its sports facilities or sports team? Did you visit a campsite or a museum in a big city? Each group's stop should be fully and enthusiastically described. If the stop is close to other attractions, describe them.

Entertainment. Does the place offer special amusements that nobody would want to miss? Give specific information about features, admission fees, and hours.

Accommodations. Where did the group stay, what did it cost, and why is it recommended to other travelers?

Food. Whether you cooked out or ate at city restaurants, tell readers about the food and how great it was.

For more information. Include a section with addresses and telephone numbers for more information about each stop.

PRINTING THE BROCHURE

Write the brochure using word processing software; use desktop publishing software to design and lay out the brochure. Be sure to use illustrations. If a scanner is not available, find some black-and-white photos to copy using a copy machine. One brochure with material from both classes should be the final product. Print several copies and distribute them to other classes, administrators, and parent groups.

Appendix: Product List

Chapters 2 and 3

The Video Encyclopedia of the 20th Century®
CEL Educational Resources
655 Third Avenue
New York, NY 10017
(212) 557-3400
(800) 235-3339

Chapter 4

WILSONLINE
H. W. Wilson
950 University Avenue
Bronx, NY 10452
(718) 588-8400
(800) 367-6770

This address is for a free class set of instructions for the *Readers' Guide to Periodical Literature.*

Chapter 5

Tom Snyder Productions, Inc.
Education Software
90 Sherman Street
Cambridge, MA 02140
(617) 876-4433
(800) 342-0236

Chapter 6

Earthquest, Inc.
125 University Avenue
Palo Alto, CA 94301
(415) 321-5838
(800) 321-8925

New Grolier Multimedia Encyclopedia
Grolier Electronic Publishing
Danbury, CT 06816
(203) 797-3500
(800) 285-4535

Chapter 7

CompuServe, Inc.
5000 Arlington Centre Blvd.
P.O. Box 20212
Columbus, OH 43220
(800) 848-8199

Chapter 8

America Online
8619 Westwood Center Drive
Vienna, VA 22182
(800) 827-6364

Index

About the Author

Norma Heller has spent much of her 20-year career as a school librarian at Intermediate School 52, one of the first schools in New York City to add computers to the library media center. As a member of New York City School Library System (NYCSLS), she has participated in cooperative collection development and developed a short story collection that is shared by libraries throughout the New York metropolitan area through interlibrary loan. Ms. Heller has provided training in the use of electronic media to other librarians, and is herself trained in the education of gifted and talented students.

Ms. Heller was awarded a grant by Community School District 8 for teaching students how to use CompuServe information network, and a student-produced videotape made in her I.S. 52 library media center won first prize for creativity in the junior high school category in a national contest sponsored by CEL Educational Resources, producers of *The Video Encyclopedia of the 20th Century*.

Ms. Heller received her M.L.S. from Pratt Institute.